THE FUTURE OF ENERGY

Technologies and Trends Driving Disruption

JASON SCHENKER

THE FUTURE OF ENERGY

Technologies and Trends Driving Disruption

BY JASON SCHENKER

·ISBN: 978-1-946197-35-1 *Paperback*
        978-1-946197-29-0 *Ebook*

For my family.

CONTENTS

CONTENTS

CONTENTS

BIG CHANGES ARE AFOOT IN THE WORLD OF ENERGY

This is a book about energy — one of the most important elements of modern society and the economy. It is also an industry in transition. There are big changes afoot in the world of energy.

At their core, many of the disruptions coming to energy are fundamental. They are being driven by the unstoppable dynamics of demographics, the force of regulatory policies, and a rising social and investor focus on renewables.

The sources of supply and demand are changing. And the mix of energy sources will be changing too.

Technology advancements are also at the heart of changes coming to energy — as is the case across all sectors.

But energy is also a sector marred by hype. This can be seen in some of the overblown expectations for renewables and electric vehicles. The hindrances to these technologies are limited by the unassailable realities of physics and chemistry.

These challenges can also be framed as physical and material science limitations.

As I have written in more than one book, every industry that wants to survive and thrive in the current era of disruption needs to take a long look in the mirror and actionably decide to become a tech industry.

And this is also true of the energy space as well.

I have been doing energy strategic planning and price forecasting for 15 years, since my time as the Chief Energy and Commodity Economist at Wachovia's investment bank, at McKinsey and Company, and in my own firm, Prestige Economics, which I founded in 2009. I have learned a lot about energy along the way. But my focus on longer-term energy topics became most pronounced when I founded The Futurist Institute in 2016.

This book represents an attempt to share what I have learned about energy — and to explore some of the most critical topics at the heart of the debate about the future of energy in its many forms.

Acknowledgements.
I want to acknowledge and thank all the people who helped make this book come together, especially **Nawfal Patel**, who managed the production of *The Future of Energy*.

Most importantly, I want to thank my family for supporting me in my education, career, entrepreneurship, and authorship.

I am always most grateful for the support of my loving wife, **Ashley Schenker**, and to my wonderful parents, **Janet and Jeffrey Schenker**.

My family supports me in countless ways by providing emotional support and editorial feedback.

Every time I write a book, it's a crazy experience that spills over into my family life, so to them and to everyone else who helped me in this process: Thank you!

Finally, thank you for buying this book.

I hope you enjoy *The Future of Energy*!

Jason Schenker
Austin, Texas
May 2019

THE FUTURE OF ENERGY

Energy is a word often used to mean many different things. In the context of this book, the subject of energy encompasses crude oil, refined products like gasoline and diesel, power, coal, natural gas, and renewable energy sources. And it also includes the business of energy from an operational standpoint.

Essentially, the term *energy* could be more concisely summed up as power and transportation fuels in all their forms, as well as the businesses associated with them..

The future of energy will be impacted by changes in critical geographic sources of energy supply and demand as well as changes in the mix of various energy consumption.

And the future of energy will be driven by technology that impacts the way data is processed, leveraged, and monetized. Automation will also drive changes in production operations, energy consumption, analytics, and across office functions.

The Structure of This Book

In order to tackle the most important factors in navigating *The Future of Energy*, I have divided this book into seven sections:

- **Energy Overview**
- **Changing Physical Markets**
- **Energy Demand-Side Technologies**
- **Energy Supply-Side Data Technologies**
- **Energy Supply-Side Physical Technologies**
- **Trends in Clean Energy and Renewables**
- **Pulling Everything Together**

In the first section of *The Future of Energy*, **Energy Overview**, I discuss why I wrote this book and the importance of spikes in Chapter 1. In Chapter 2, I discuss the importance of technology and energy, especially as it relates to the value of formal education and having a learning process.

In the second section, **Changing Physical Markets**, I discuss some of the changes in global oil and natural gas supply and demand dynamics — as well as some of the changes coming in the global energy mix. In Chapter 3, I discuss the future of oil supply, and in Chapter 4 I discuss the future of oil demand. In Chapter 5 and Chapter 6, I discuss the future of natural gas supply and natural gas demand, respectively. Finally, in Chapter 7, I discuss the outlook for the changing energy mix on a domestic and global basis.

The third section of this book is about **Energy Demand-Side Technologies**, which includes discussions of some of the most important technology touchstones that are likely to impact — or are perceived to likely impact — energy demand dynamics. This section kicks off in Chapter 8, where I write about electric vehicles. In Chapter 9, the focus is on e-commerce.

This section also includes a discussion of two other big dynamics that are likely to impact energy in the decades to come. On the downside for energy demand is the question of telecommuting, which is the subject of Chapter 10. And in Chapter 11, I discuss the changes that are likely to accompany smart power, meters, and grids.

In the fifth section of the book, I examine **Energy Supply-Side Data Technologies**. This includes an examination of data topics like predictive analytics, machine learning, and AI, in Chapter 12. In Chapter 13, I discuss the potential ramifications and importance of quantum computing for the supply side of energy markets. Thereafter, in Chapter 14, I discuss blockchain potential for the energy space.

Energy Supply-Side Physical Technologies are the focus of the sixth section of this book. This section looks at some important emerging technologies that are likely to impact corporate activities in the office, as opposed to in the oil patch or at power assets. I broadly discuss automation in Chapter 15, and I discuss operational drones in Chapter 16.

Trends in Clean Energy and Renewables is the focus of the seventh section of this book. This section includes a sweeping overview of the upside potential as well as the physical and material science limitations of some clean energy and renewable technologies. In Chapter 17, there is a focus on and discussion of clean power, climate change, and CO_2.

Thereafter, I discuss wind power in Chapter 18. I discuss solar power in Chapter 19. In Chapter 20, I discuss hydroelectric and geothermal power. In Chapter 21, I examine waste to energy, and in Chapter 22 I discuss hydrogen fuel cell technology. In Chapter 23, I examine the state of ethanol and ethanol vehicles, which currently comprise an outright majority of U.S. alternative vehicles. Finally, in Chapter 24, I visit the subject of nuclear power generation.

Many of the clean and renewable forms of energy face significant limitations. But they are likely to become increasingly important parts of the energy mix of the future. However, renewable energy is unlikely to replace hydrocarbon energy completely.

This is a subject of Chapter 5, which focuses on the future energy mix. But it is also a subject of the final section of the book, **Pulling Everything Together**, which also includes the book's conclusion.

In that final section of *The Future of Energy*, I tie in themes shared throughout this book in order to present some important cohesive expectations of the big changes coming to energy in the decade ahead — and beyond.

Energy is an important driver of macroeconomic growth. It is critical for the global supply chain. And it will be changing in the decade ahead. But the changes coming are likely to be unexpected, because too much emphasis has been placed on some trends, with others being completely ignored.

The topics in this book should provide an entrée into the field of energy as well as an overview of the field of futurist thought. For the curious reader, there will be many more topics to explore in both fields.

Energy Overview

CHAPTER 1

WHY I WROTE THIS BOOK

I wrote this book to add context to the debate and discourse around the future of energy.

Energy has been a foundational subject for my professional development, and it is a topic I have spent a significant portion of my career covering, at both tactical and strategic levels.

I have been making forecasts about energy prices as well as industry trends for 15 years. And this represents my first attempt to reconcile these two outlooks into a comprehensive and sober outlook of the challenges, opportunities, hype, and hope for the future of energy.

In some respects, I started covering energy almost by accident, 15 years ago, in early 2004. I was a newly minted economist at the then third-largest bank in the United States, Wachovia, which became part of Wells Fargo in the wake of the financial crisis during the Great Recession.

Although I was initially tasked with covering inflation, industrials, and international topics, oil prices became a critical factor at the intersection of those topics at the start of my career.

You see, in early 2004, the price of oil was rising and driving inflation higher. At the time, the global economy had improved significantly in the years since the 2001 recession. And the global economy was poised for further expansionary growth. Oil prices began rising sharply, and this presented a threat to inflation. At the intersection of inflation, industrials, and international economics was the price of crude.

Econometric forecast models I built at the time supported the price-bullish narrative of strong macroeconomic fundamentals of global economic expansion against a backdrop of protracted oil and gas underinvestment.

Although I was somewhat new stepping up to the plate, the Chief Economist of Wachovia gave me a wide berth and the leeway to build models and make forecasts about the price of crude oil. I made some bold forecasts in early 2004, predicting that WTI crude oil prices could close above $50 per barrel before the end of the year, and I noted further upside risks beyond that.

At the time, it was a scandalous forecast. Reporters from major media networks called me on the phone. And they laughed.

But on 28 September 2004, WTI crude oil prices rose above $50 for the first time. The next day, I had a new job title: Chief Energy Economist of the bank.

Thus began a 15-year career in covering energy topics from oil and natural gas to power and renewables. In the time immediately following my success with forecasting crude oil prices, I codified and expanded energy and commodity market research coverage at Wachovia. Because of my role within the investment bank, I had the good fortune to see oil and gas, power, wind, and even biofuels deals. In some instances, I supported and performed due diligence on those energy deals.

From a policy and macroeconomic perspective, during my time in banking, which lasted until late 2007, oil prices became a critical driver of inflationary pressures and Fed forecasts. Although oil prices peaked in mid-2008, and fell thereafter, they have remained a hot topic in business media and financial market discussions. The energy market volatility and global macro exposure has made crude oil a much more important topic for investment allocation decisions than before 2004.

As a hot topic for investors and policymakers, oil prices — and anything energy related — are likely to remain important points of discussion. This is also true as the discourse around the topic of climate change becomes more pronounced.

These are just some of the reasons why examining the future of energy is important. Changes that are coming will have big implications for corporations, industries, and entire economies.

Fortunately, my experiences in banking — and my subsequent experiences in consulting — have helped me see a broad swath of the energy world.

When the financial crisis was approaching, I left banking and joined McKinsey as a Risk Specialist to build commodity trading desks, design risk management and hedging strategies, and advise energy trading firms.

In that role, I was fortunate enough to have had the opportunity to provide content direction on projects related to all parts of the oil supply chain, from upstream oil and gas exploration and production (so-called E&P) to midstream projects with refiners, pipelines, and utilities. I even directed downstream projects with critical energy consumers in manufacturing, chemical, and transportation sectors.

All of these sectors will face fundamental challenges in the decade ahead. And some will fare better than others.

In my own firm, Prestige Economics, which I founded in 2009, I have been forecasting oil and gas prices — and I have been ranked #1 in the world by Bloomberg News for my price forecast accuracy for WTI crude oil, Brent crude oil, and Henry Hub natural gas price forecasts. And during that time, I also completed the Energy Risk Professional™ designation from the Global Association of Risk Professionals to further my corporate knowledge of energy and power in all of their forms — and all of the associated risks.

While I have been doing energy price forecasting and strategic planning since my time at Wachovia and McKinsey, my focus on longer-term energy topics became most pronounced when I founded The Futurist Institute.

I even created and recorded a course called The Future of Energy as part of our Certified Futurist and Long-Term Analyst™ designation, which is also known as the FLTA™.

As in the eponymous course from The Futurist Institute, it is my goal in this book on *The Future of Energy* to incorporate my knowledge of markets, the energy supply chain, and new and emerging technologies into an integrated set of expectations for energy in the coming decade — and beyond.

It is my hope that this book will become your first stop on a long journey to learn more about energy markets, corporations, opportunities, and limitations.

Now, let's get to it!

CHAPTER 2

TECHNOLOGY AND ENERGY

As I have written in more than one book, every industry that wants to survive and thrive in the current era of disruption needs to take a long look in the mirror and actionably decide to become a tech industry at its core.

Technology is and will be a critical element of corporate success.

And this is just as true in the oil patch as it is for companies that manufacture computer hardware or software.

Let me share a story that drives this point home.

In 2005, I attended my first OPEC meeting — something I still do on a regular basis. Showing up is a critical element of making forecasts and futurist predictions. The intersection of energy and technology became fully apparent to me when I attended an OPEC meeting in November 2016.

It was the meeting where OPEC and non-OPEC members came to an agreement to reduce their oil production levels to support oil prices.

But before the OPEC members got to this landmark decision, they discussed the new OPEC app. It was like something out of the television show *Silicon Valley*, with talk of the app's UI/UX (user interface / user experience) functionality. It was honestly a bit surreal, given the potential for such a monumental meeting.

I captured this discussion in Vienna, Austria, in the picture in Figure 2-1.

Figure 2-1: OPEC App Launch

I often use this image when giving presentations about energy and technology — and especially when talking to energy companies about technology. It resonates because OPEC is not often thought of as a forward-thinking innovator in the energy world.

It is, after all, an organization that is now over 50 years old. And yet, despite this perception of OPEC as an older organization and NGO, it has made great strides in producing more sophisticated analyses of global energy markets. And this moment with OPEC in the spotlight — a moment when it chose to discuss and debut its app — highlighted its embrace of technology.

And it set an example that other energy firms would be wise not to overlook.

After all, if OPEC can take a few moments to delay what was arguably its most important decision in history in order to discuss its technology initiative, private energy companies should focus on the importance of technology as well.

Changing Physical Markets

CHAPTER 3

FUTURE OIL SUPPLY DYNAMICS

The future dynamics of oil supply will change. And these changes are likely to succeed the changes of recent years that we have seen during the so-called shale revolution.

Until the late 2000s, almost all crude oil was extracted from vertical oil wells. These wells were drilled more or less straight down (hence the name, vertically) into underground pockets of oil. Some people also call these conventional oil wells.

In the late 2000s, however, the oil drilling game experienced a significant change. Following an era of unprecedented high oil prices, which reached a zenith in July 2008, more work was being done to extract oil from shale plays. This, however, required a different kind of oil well. It required a well that could be drilled down and then horizontally. This can be seen in Figure 3-1.

Horizontal oil drilling requires more technology and precision than most conventional wells. And it requires water and sand to perform something called hydraulic fracturing — or "fracking."

The fracking process gets its name from the physical process used to extract oil from a shale rock formation. In sum, fracking requires creating actual fractures in the shale rock formation where oil or gas hydrocarbons are located.

Although fracking has been a critical and essential technology to bolstering U.S. oil and gas exploration and production over the past decade, it has been around since the 1860s — although the first forms of a more modern kind of fracking came into existence in the 1940s, with the kind of fracking we have today not emerging until the 1990s.[1] But despite a long history of this technology, we didn't see this technology really take flight until it began to be applied at scale in the mid-to-late 2000s, as the price of oil was approaching all-time highs.

Figure 3-1: Shale Oil Drilling[2]

The knock-on effects from a protracted period of post-oil-crisis underinvestment paired with unprecedented global growth sent oil prices sharply higher in the mid-2000s. And in that context of higher prices, oil and gas became a more attractive space for investment dollars. And one of the new technologies to help avert the potential decline portended as peak oil was the potential for horizontal drilling combined with fracking technology.

This was effective in a number of what became known as unconventional plays. So you know, a *play* in the parlance of the oil and gas world demotes a region where oil is located. And while there are many potential shale oil plays across the globe, some of the most wildly fruitful shale plays have been in the United States. These are shown in Figure 3-2.

Figure 3-2: Future Oil Supply[3]

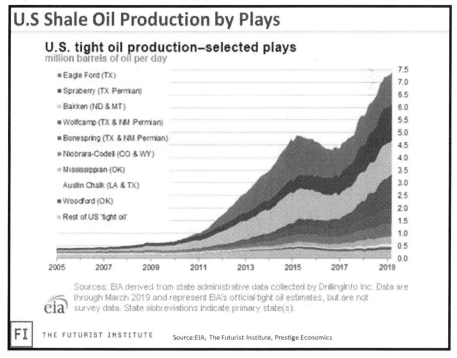

The reason I've spent a great deal of time laying out some of the fundamentals of the shale oil revolution, as it has come to be called, is that shale oil will continue to be critical for oil supplies in the decade ahead.

Interestingly, because shale oil is much cheaper to extract than deep-sea oil or by refining oil sands in Canada, shale oil has come to occupy an enviable position in the oil production cost curve. This can be seen in an illustrative fashion in Figure 3-3.

Now, a cost curve shows how much oil costs to produce for a certain volume. And some of the cheapest oil in the world arguably comes from some OPEC member countries as well as some parts of Russia (if we exclude the cost of the oil export tax).

Figure 3-3: Prestige Economics Illustrative Cost Curve of Oil

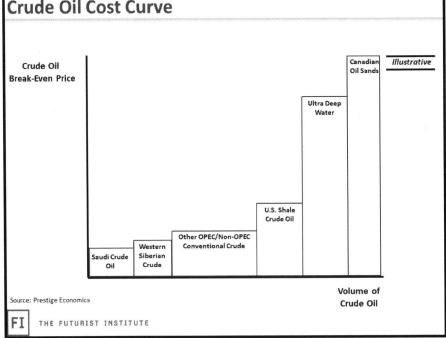

Essentially, what you see in Figure 3-3 is that U.S. shale oil is neither the cheapest nor the most expensive oil to extract in the world. This means that the United States now occupies what some people have deemed a swing producer. I think this terminology is a bit of a misnomer, especially when we talk about oil production from large national oil companies — or NOCs — like the members of OPEC. After all, the term *swing producer* implies a singular decision-making or action-taking process. And the U.S. oil patch is anything but singular. There are countless U.S. oil and gas companies, investment firms, and other assorted entities that are drilling for shale oil.

But the notion of swing producer does ring true in one respect: It implies that U.S. shale oil can ramp up and down, depending on oil prices and demand. Since shale oil is relatively abundant, and it isn't the most expensive oil to drill, it will be a critical source of additional marginal barrels of crude oil.

So, if you equate the term *swing producer* with the idea of significant producers of additional marginal barrels of oil at profitable levels, then maybe the term would fit.

Even in 2019, I have been forecasting that between 1.5 and 2 million barrels of additional shale oil production will be added to the global oil supply. And millions and millions more barrels of daily U.S. shale oil production are coming in the decade ahead.

This is one of the most critical changes coming to the future of oil supply: The United States has come to occupy a critical place in the global oil supply chain as a producer of marginal barrels.

For many decades, the United States had been a major source of U.S. crude oil demand. It had been a massive net importer of crude oil — something I will discuss in the following chapter.

But now, the United States has come to occupy a position as the fulcrum in the global oil supply chain. Relatively cheap U.S. natural gas and power have also helped fuel the growing refinery business on the U.S. Gulf Coast. In fact, the U.S. Gulf Coast even became a net exporter of crude oil in 2018, as can be seen in Figure 3-4.

And the United States will become an increasingly important source of U.S. refined products in the decade ahead.

Figure 3-4: U.S. Gulf Coast Net Exports[4]

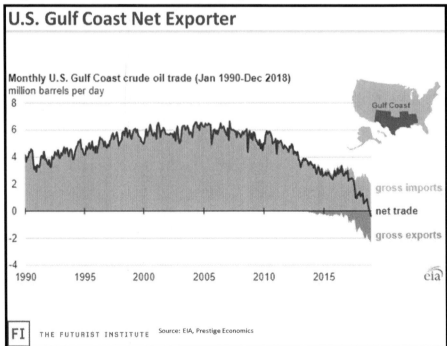

Risks Ahead

Shale oil production has proven fruitful, and drilling for both oil and gas has expanded across plays significantly in the past decade and a half. But there are some risks ahead, including limits to the upside on future production.

The biggest risk is that shale oil production will suffer from what's known in the industry as a steep decline curve. So you know, a decline curve shows the decline in the production levels of an oil or gas well. And the steep decline curve in shale wells in means that the production of oil and gas from a horizontal shale oil well would be likely to deplete rapidly. Generally, speaking, this is not something that was an issue for vertical wells. But it is for shale oil production.

Allow me, for a brief moment, to frame this situation with an analogy. Maybe you've heard of the television show *The Beverly Hillbillies*. The tale hinges on the notion that the patriarch of the family accidentally found oil while he was out hunting. The asset provided long-lived wealth for the family and allowed them to move to Beverly Hills.

Although never a very plausible story to begin with, this would be beyond any realm of the imaginable for shale oil. After all, shale oil drilling — rather than hinging on the luck of a stray bullet — requires massive technical skill and drilling a well down thousands of feet vertically before making the drill take a 90-degree turn to drill horizontally before fracking can even begin.

While it is generally true that long-lived conventional oil assets drilled with vertical wells could prove a long-term income stream, the same is not true for shale oil wells. Because of those steep decline curves, you would need to drill and drill and drill to secure a long-term income stream.

The price of Beverly Hills real estate aside, the biggest problem with a post-shale-revolution adaptation of such a story is that because of the steep decline curves associated with unconventional shale oil wells, you would essentially need to perpetually increase the number of wells you drill to maintain your level of production at a flat level.

At some point, this could become a problem for the future of shale oil as the realities of U.S. production and limits of plays bump up against something known as *the law of large numbers*.

In short, the problem of decline curves will only become more critical as the number of shale oil wells increase. And at some point, the sheer number of wells will make the replacement of crude oil lost to eroding decline curves essentially insurmountable. This isn't an issue for the next five years, but 10 years from now, it could become a bigger issue.

An associated risk for future production that is impacted by steep decline curves of shale oil wells is that shale oil wells could also become less profitable as maximum well yields potentially fall as drilling occurs farther away from areas with the greatest yield — areas that are known as *pay zones*.

The potential for lower profitability, coupled with steep decline curves, threatens to eventually put a ceiling on the amount of U.S. shale oil supply that can be reasonably extracted.

And at some point, this could actually present downside risks to overall U.S. crude oil production.

On a global basis, the risks are a bit different. As you may be aware, shale oil and gas plays exist all over the world. This can be seen in Figure 3-5.

But there is also a risk that shale oil production may not be as productive — or may not have as nearly as high an ROI — in other countries as it has been in the United States.

Figure 3-5: Future Oil Supply[5]

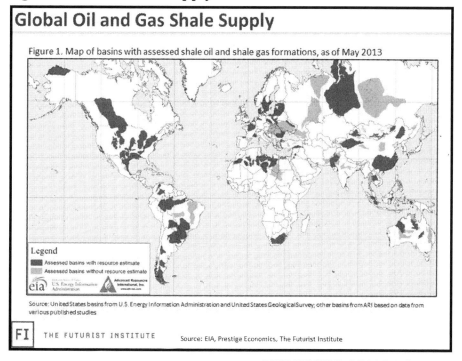

One big benefit is that U.S. shale oil is close to a major end market.

After all, the U.S. summer driving season has global price implications, even though U.S. crude oil imports have drastically fallen in recent years.

A second big plus for U.S. shale oil production is existing U.S. infrastructure.

The use of U.S. pipelines, refineries, rail, and other infrastructure — although challenging at times for the shale boom — are still likely to prove more easily leveraged for transporting both shale oil and shale gas.

A lack of infrastructure abroad would present significant challenges in terms of transporting and monetizing the value of those otherwise currently trapped hydrocarbons.

For many years, there was talk in the oil patch about the handful of rigs that were drilling in Continental Europe for shale oil and gas but with little success.

Looking Ahead
In the coming decade, the United States will occupy an increasingly critical position of the fulcrum in global energy markets. This will be driven by its relatively cost-effective refinery capacity, its broad-based infrastructure that can tap shale assets, its deep capital markets, and the increase of its petroleum product and crude oil export levels.

While a likely continuation of OPEC and non-OPEC production collaboration will remain critical from an aggregated global oil supply and pricing policy standpoint, U.S. crude oil production will ascend farther in terms of pricing influence. This is especially true as we consider that U.S. shale oil barrels are likely to remain the most abundant sources of potential additional marginal barrels at scale.

While the 2000s were the oil decade and the 2010s were a decade of recovery, the 2020s are likely to be a decade of greater American influence for supply in the global energy supply chain than at any point in history.

And this is likely to prove just as true for natural gas as it is for crude oil.

CHAPTER 4

FUTURE OIL DEMAND DYNAMICS

Electric vehicles are the biggest topic when most people think of oil demand — and it's a bearish factor that they consider. But they are overlooking one critical factor: Global wealth is rising, and petroleum-fueled vehicles are going to become more important with the expansion of emerging market middle classes.

And this means that the locus critical oil demand is also going to shift from the OECD to the Far East and other emerging markets.

In the same way that U.S. shale oil production presents a dynamic shift in terms of the geographic source of additional marginal barrels of crude oil, the rise of the middle class in emerging markets presents a similar risk for the future of marginal additional oil demand.

This means that while the 2020s are likely to be a decade in which U.S. crude oil production and refineries play an increasing role in the global supply chain of crude oil, it is also likely to be a decade in which Chinese, Indian, and other Asian demand rises drastically.

The most important thing to know is that the rise in future oil demand is being driven by fundamentals. Most important among these is that the global population will increase by over 2 billion people through 2050, with almost 800 million being added in the coming decade.[1] You can see this in World Bank population forecasts through 2050 in Figure 4-1.

On top of this significant increase in global population, there will also be a significant rise in real GDP per capita in the decades ahead. In Figure 4-2, you can see the difference between real GDP per capita in 2017 and OPEC's forecasts for 2040. This means that this per capita GDP rise will impact not just the people here now but also the 1.4 billion net new global citizens who will be added to the population through 2040.[2]

Figure 4-1: Expected Global Population Growth[3]

Future Population by Region (Millions)						
Country Name	2018	2020	2030	2040	2050	2050-2018
Europe & Central Asia	918	922	929	927	920	2
Least Development Countries	1,026	1,074	1,334	1,619	1,917	891
OECD Members	1,307	1,319	1,367	1,397	1,413	106
World	7,611	7,770	8,516	9,172	9,734	2,123

Source: Worldbank

FI THE FUTURIST INSTITUTE

As we consider the rise in real per capita GDP growth, it is important to note that China is likely to see the biggest rise, with India likely to be a close second. The concept of the 21st century as the "Asian century" has been postulated by a number of economists and analysts. And that fundamental reality of massively increasing Asian economic wealth is something that will have a truly significant impact on oil demand growth.

But Asia isn't the only source of rising demand; OPEC member countries, the Middle East and Africa, and Latin America will also be critical. It's really in OECD countries, which are developed economies, where we expect decreases in oil demand growth. In fact, OPEC data and reports note that OECD oil demand growth peaked back in 2005.

Figure 4-2: Real GDP per Capita[4]

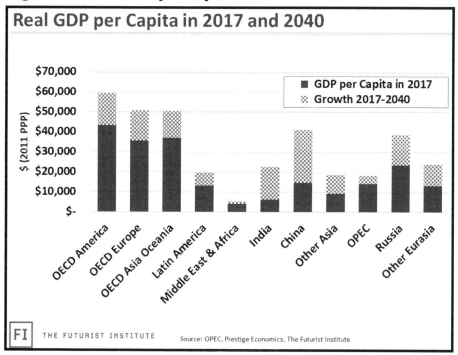

But the rise in the pace of annual oil demand growth, however, is also expected to slow overall. In Figure 4-3, you can see OPEC oil demand growth forecasts through 2023. The pace of annual growth for the world is poised to slow — even in the next few years, especially as OECD oil demand growth turns negative.

Yet even though the pace of growth is poised to slow, the level of global oil consumption is still likely to rise for many years to come. And it should come as no surprise that transportation fuels are the key source of demand. According to OPEC analysis in Figure 4-4, the rise in demand will occur across a broad range of products, with demand for light products, like gasoline, as well as middle distillates, like diesel, likely to rise significantly through 2023.

Figure 4-3: Oil Demand Growth by Region Through 2023[5]

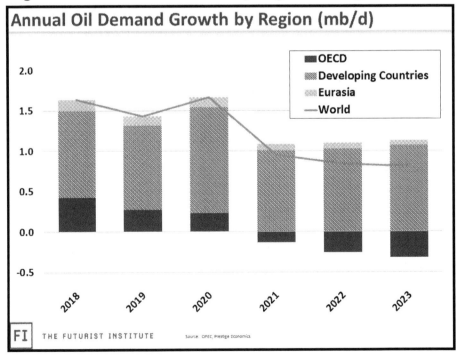

Some might say here that OPEC is talking their book. This is a phrase people on Wall Street like to say when an analyst makes a forecast that could benefit the traders on the same desk or at the same companies. The argument here would be that OPEC countries produce oil, so they want to show a rise in demand, and that we should discount these forecasts.

But I disagree because it doesn't make a lot of sense. OPEC countries don't hold trading positions they are waiting to exit, like a hedge fund or bank trading desk. OPEC countries and their respective NOCs, as well as the independent oil companies — or IOCs — they partner with, are in fundamentally long positions because crude oil exists within OPEC country borders.

Figure 4-4: Oil Demand Growth by Product Through 2023[6]

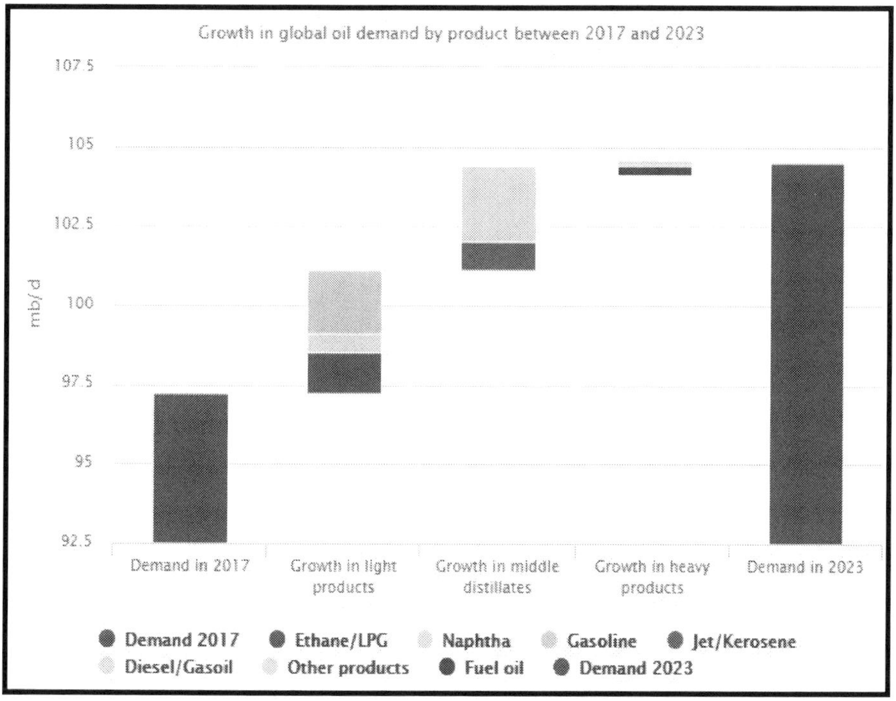

If anything, I think OPEC may actually be more bearish about crude oil expectations, given that OPEC forecasts of electric vehicle penetration is more aggressive than U.S. EIA forecasts.

At the end of the day, whether the OPEC numbers turn out to be exactly precise or not, one thing is true: They are based on economic fundamentals of global growth, middle class wealth, and supply chain needs that will accompany that rise in wealth. In other words, like it or not, this is likely to be directionally how the future oil demand scenario plays out. Plus, these forecasts of oil demand growth also represent a continuation of a trend of rising emerging market wealth and oil demand — rather than the beginning of a new trend or a break from a trend.

Figure 4-5: Annual Gross Crude Oil Imports[7]

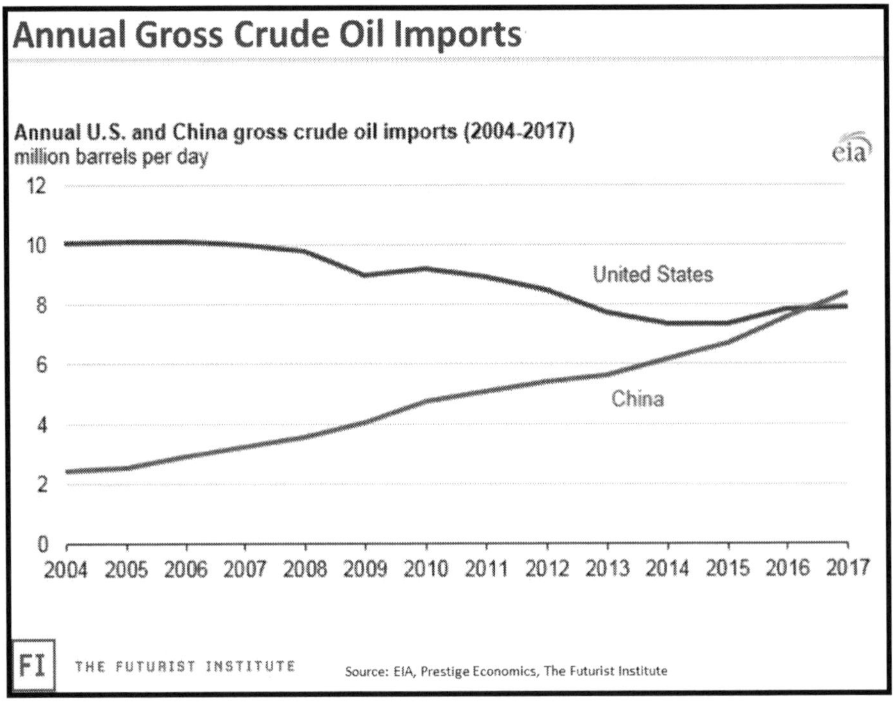

Annual Gross Crude Oil Imports

Annual U.S. and China gross crude oil imports (2004-2017)
million barrels per day

eia

United States

China

2004 2005 2006 2007 2008 2009 2010 2011 2012 2013 2014 2015 2016 2017

FI THE FUTURIST INSTITUTE Source: EIA, Prestige Economics, The Futurist Institute

In Figure 4-5, you can see the historical trend of Chinese and U.S. gross crude oil imports. While U.S. crude oil imports began declining in the mid-to-late 2000s, Chinese gross imports have almost quadrupled since 2004. Besides the trend in gross oil imports, net oil imports in the United States have declined even more significantly because of the U.S. export of crude oil — especially from the Gulf Coast, as I noted in the previous chapter.

Against that backdrop of declining U.S. gross oil imports and further falling net oil imports, China has seen its net imports increase. In fact, China has been the single biggest net importer of crude oil in the world since 2012. Looking ahead, China is likely to become a bigger net importer, while the United States is likely to become a smaller one.

Figure 4-6: U.S. and China Net Crude Oil Imports[8]

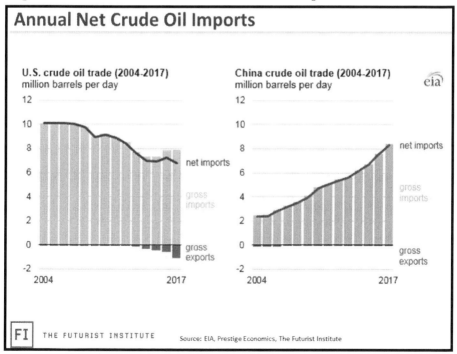

Because of the importance of Chinese demand for oil in absolute terms, the Chinese economy has become more critical for the price of crude oil. For years, we have watched various national manufacturing purchasing managers indices — or PMIs — for implications about the future growth in individual countries.

But because the Chinese economy is so fundamentally critical for the price of crude oil, the pace of Chinese manufacturing, which is a critical part of the Chinese economy, is a critical data point to watch for implications as to the strength or weakness of crude oil prices. From 2014 through 2016, crude oil prices collapsed globally. Fingers were pointed at the shale oil revolution and the rise of supply. But oil wasn't the only commodity that fell during that time period. Almost every commodity price fell.

Figure 4-7: Chinese Caixin Manufacturing PMI[9]

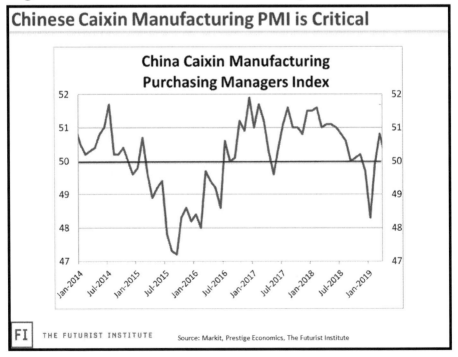

And that had nothing to do with shale oil!

The main driver of oil prices — and other commodity prices that fell so hard from late 2014 until mid-2016 — was a Chinese manufacturing recession that lasted from December 2014 until June 2016. You can see that recession in Figure 4-7, which shows the Chinese Caixin Manufacturing PMI. This is, in my opinion, the single most important data release that comes out of China every month. That was the main driver.

That Chinese manufacturing recession easily explains how commodities as disparate as steel, tin, aluminum, rubber, nickel, copper, lead, zinc, iron ore, and oil all came under pressure and collapsed from late 2014 through the first half of 2016. And the rebound in the Caixin thereafter helps explain the rise in those commodity prices thereafter — until the Caixin weakened in 2018 and 2019.

An important takeaway here should also be that over the coming decade, Chinese, Indian, and other emerging market data for manufacturing and economic growth will become increasingly important for oil prices. After all, if emerging markets are the sources of ever-greater rising additional marginal demand of crude oil, those will be the areas where the data would be most likely to impact crude oil prices. And this will remain especially true for China and the privately compiled Chinese Caixin Manufacturing PMI because China is likely to remain the world's largest gross and net importer in the decade ahead. And its gross and net import volumes are likely to rise significantly.

Looking Ahead

In the past decade, China has become a critical source of oil demand. Now, looking ahead, the rise in emerging market real GDP per capita portends a massive rise in oil demand growth in China, India, and emerging Asia (as well as other emerging markets) as personal and commercial consumption of fuels rise significantly. In the coming decade, Asia will become an even more important source of oil demand.

Some other shifts of the past decade are unlikely to reverse in the coming decade either. One example is the transatlantic arbitrage, which you can see in Figure 4-8. The so-called TAA existed as a financial manifestation of physical demand flows, with WTI crude oil prices trading consistently at a premium over Brent prices.

Figure 4-8: The Transatlantic Arbitrage[10]

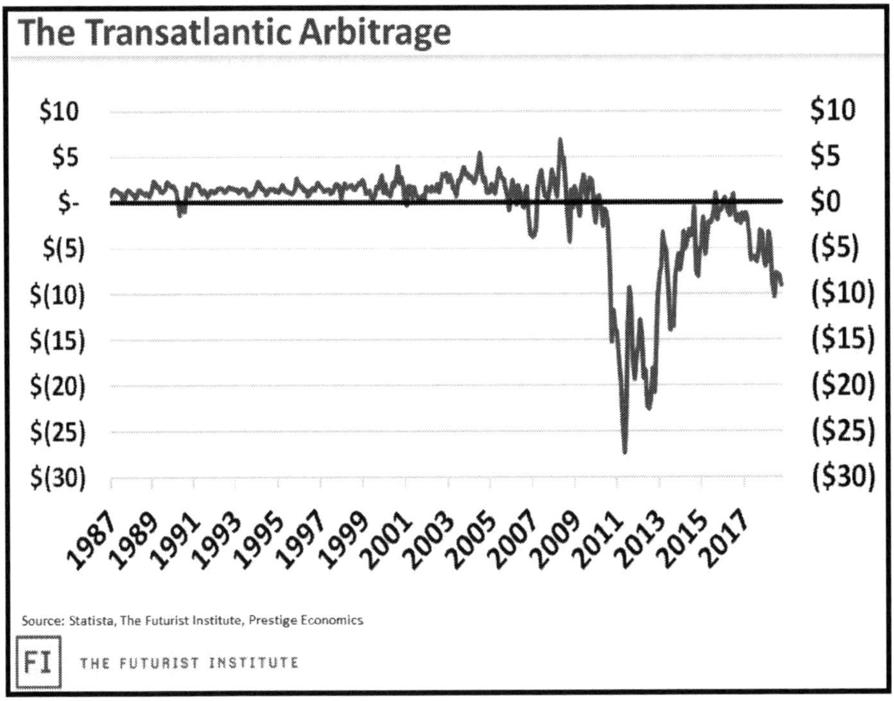

The Transatlantic Arbitrage

Source: Statista, The Futurist Institute, Prestige Economics

FI THE FUTURIST INSTITUTE

That made sense for a very long time. After all, if the United States was the biggest physical net short position for crude oil in the world, the price of WTI would need to be higher than Brent in order to attract the physical flows (and cover the transport costs) of a similar grade of crude in another location.

That's a simple arbitrage trade: Buy the crude in the North Sea, put it in a tanker, and offload it at Cushing. In theory the TAA should at least cover the transport cost — if not more for the hassle of transporting the crude and associated risks involved.

But as U.S. imports have fallen and U.S. crude and product exports have risen, that net short position is less critical.

Plus, crude oil supplies have essentially become trapped at Cushing, and with WTI crude oil as a physically settled crude oil contract, there is more risk than with Brent contracts, which can be financially settled.

This means that the preference for Brent over WTI as a means of hedging and speculating is likely to remain. And even from a purely physical flow standpoint, it means that WTI may continue to trade at a discount to Brent crude oil prices for the foreseeable future in the decade ahead.

In short, it won't just be the sources of new and rising demand that impact oil prices. The physical realities that began setting in during the past decade will continue to impact the most critical arbitrage opportunities between the two main benchmarks in the decade ahead.

CHAPTER 5

FUTURE NATURAL GAS SUPPLY DYNAMICS

The United States has been the world's top producer of natural gas since 2009. And as we look at the decade ahead, U.S. consumption — and global consumption of natural gas — is going to rise. U.S. production will increase for domestic market use as there is a shift for power generation away from coal. And there will also be a massive shift toward LNG exports in coming years.

As with crude oil, U.S. shale natural gas production has been revolutionary. But the impact on natural gas supplies has been — and is likely to continue to be — even larger than the impact on crude oil markets. As one executive at a client company in the natural gas business told me almost a decade ago, "There is quite a bit of shale oil, but shale natural gas is everywhere."

The head of a client trading desk once described the situation in the natural gas market and the price outlook as one in which prices could be low "forever." I think at some point, prices will rise, but they have been low for years. And sharp moves higher may be years away.

Even though shale natural gas may not exactly be "everywhere," it is abundant. U.S. oil and gas shale plays can be seen in Figure 5-1. Although drilling has increased across plays, as noted in Chapter 3, there is a lot more gas that can be drilled.

For the moment, some of the shale gas that could be extracted from more remote plays is trapped. Unlike oil, natural gas cannot be easily trucked away or put on rail cars. And so, some trapped gas is exceptionally cheap, while infrastructure lags behind production. But that will change. This was actually the focus of a major natural gas forecasting and consulting project for an Asian consumer of natural gas and hopeful recipient of U.S. LNG. If we fast-forward a number of decades, we see a more integrated U.S. natural gas market, with shale being more critical.

Figure 5-1: Shale Oil and Gas Plays[1]

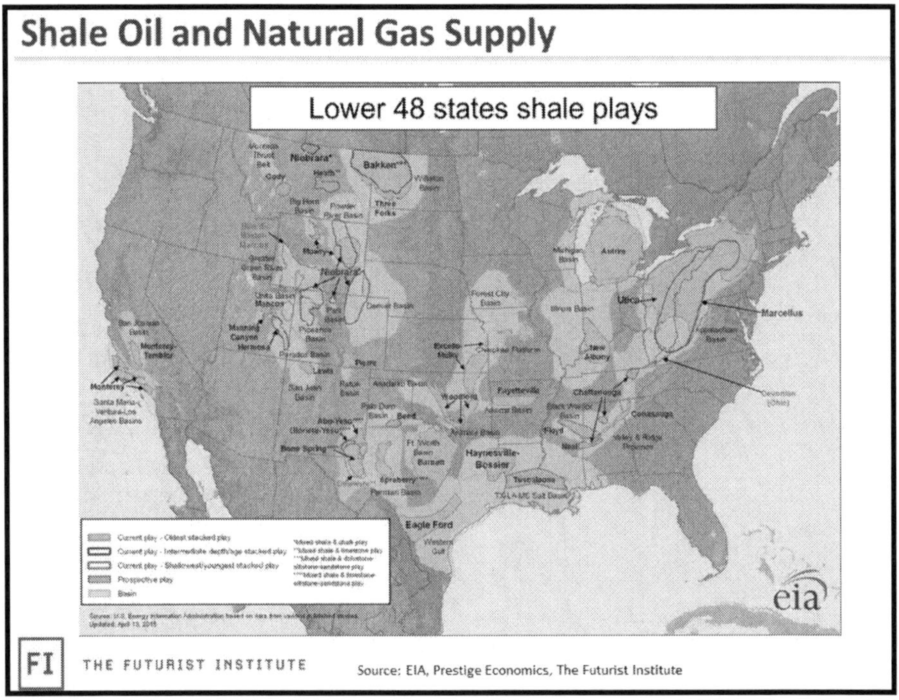
Shale Oil and Natural Gas Supply
Lower 48 states shale plays
Bakken
Niobrara
Utica
Marcellus
Haynesville-Bossier
Eagle Ford
eia
FI
THE FUTURIST INSTITUTE
Source: EIA, Prestige Economics, The Futurist Institute

Trapped natural gas is a really unfortunate problem, especially in the Marcellus and Utica plays, which are close to large urban centers, like New York and Chicago, that experience major spikes in natural gas demand during the winter. The difference in prices of natural gas between locations and as compared to the Henry Hub benchmark is called a *basis differential.*

In the dead of winter during major snowstorms natural gas prices in New York and Chicago can be many multiples of the price of natural gas prices trading on the NYMEX that use Henry Hub as the benchmark. And yet, some natural gas that is not too far away physically from New York City may be trading at a fraction of the price of the benchmark. This is a function of supply and demand in the U.S. natural gas market.

Figure 5-2: U.S. Shale Natural Gas Supply Forecast[2]

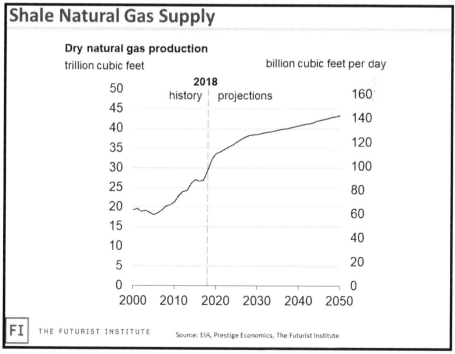

In cities, demand is high when it is cold. There are physical capacity limitations, and that drives up the price of natural gas. But isolated gas may be cheap — or it may even be flared. In other words, it is just burned for nothing.

This problem, however, could get worse before it gets better. U.S. natural gas production is poised to rise significantly in the coming decade, which is reflected in the EIA forecast shown in Figure 5-2. This is because gas supply is generated when gas wells are drilled — and because associated gas is often produced in oil wells, where the gas molecules are associated with the oil.

Looking Ahead

Over time, the value of the massive inefficiencies in U.S. natural gas markets will be arbitraged with the addition of more pipeline capacity. But it could take decades to fully link isolated natural gas plays and major centers of demand — or at least link the more isolated gas and the broader U.S. natural gas pipeline network that can help supply meet demand, even if that demand turns out to be overseas and will be satisfied only by exporting natural gas in a liquified form as LNG.

The changes in the decade ahead may be more incremental. More pipeline capacity will be added, more gas will find a home, and more natural gas will be exported. Over the coming decade, we predict that U.S. LNG exports could reach around 20 Bcf per day. That could have a significantly supportive price impact on natural gas in the latter half of the decade ahead. But for the next few years, the abundance of shale gas could keep U.S. prices depressed even if official EIA inventories are relatively low.

This is because shale gas in uncompleted wells is assumed. The off balance sheet nature of the supply has not gone ignored in the trading world, although this has primarily depressed the benchmark price. It has had virtually no impact on the life-or-death, demand-driven spot price of natural gas at New York Citygate or Chicago Citygate during a blizzard.

On a global basis, more natural gas will be coming to market through a mix of increased production as well as LNG exports from Australia, OPEC members, and individual countries with massive, still-largely-undeveloped fields like Mozambique.

There is plenty of natural gas out there. And it's a good thing too. The turn away from coal power generation is going to drive natural gas demand because natural gas emits almost half as much CO_2 as coal power.[3] Natty, as folks in the oil and gas industry affectionately refer to natural gas, may not be renewable, but it's a lot cleaner than coal on an emissions basis.

CHAPTER 6

FUTURE NATURAL GAS
DEMAND DYNAMICS

Natural gas demand is going to rise sharply in the coming decade. In addition to the global wealth dynamics and power needs that are also driving up expected levels of crude oil consumption, there are also CO_2 policies that will drive additional natural gas demand.

As with crude oil and petroleum products, the United States will be ground zero as a critical source of additional future supplies — not just for domestic consumption but also for global natural gas needs, especially in Asia, where natural gas prices have been much higher than U.S. or even European natural gas prices in recent years.

Although I will spend more time discussing changes in the energy mix in the next chapter and CO_2 toward the end of the book, it is important to know that while natural gas produces half as much CO_2 as coal, the overall global demand for natural gas is poised to rise sharply as emerging markets experience strong growth in the decade ahead. This will make CO_2 abatement on a global scale very difficult.

We expect the biggest source of additional marginal natural gas demand in the coming decade will be China, with its demand rising by around 7.5 Tcf between 2020 and 2030, which you can see in Figure 6-1. As with demand for crude oil, we also expect significant rises in natural gas consumption in India, emerging Asia, and other emerging markets.

As the global demand for natural gas increases, U.S. LNG will become a more viable and attractive option from a trading arbitrage standpoint. In Figure 6-2, you can see the price differentials for natural gas in 2018. U.S. prices were significantly lower than prices in Asia, with an even more deeply discounted benchmark price at Henry Hub, which is physically close to current and planned Gulf Coast liquefaction facilities.

Figure 6-1: Global Natural Gas Demand Growth 2020-2030[1]

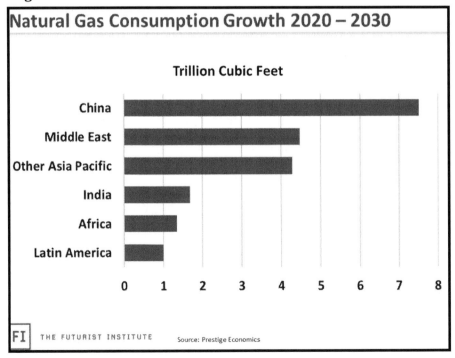

Figure 6-2: Global Natural Gas Prices in 2018[2]

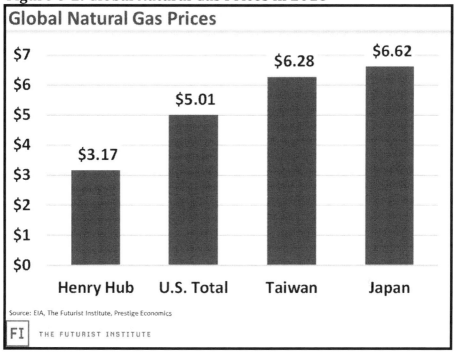

Figure 6-3: U.S. Electricity Power Sources[3]

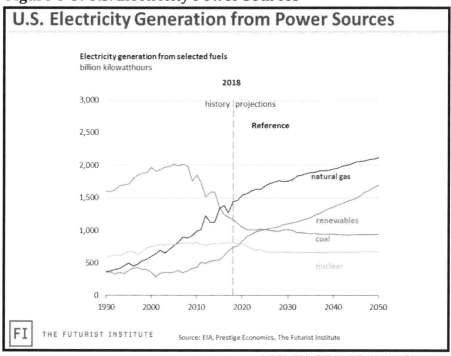

Looking Ahead

We see significant increases in global natural gas demand. And we see the United States becoming a major LNG exporter. We expect wealth as well as policy-induced demand drivers to drive this globally expanding market. Power is a fundamental economic ingredient, and we see natural gas as a preferred energy source.

This has already begun to play out in the United States, where natural gas demand currently exceeds coal demand for power generation. And we expect that this trend will accelerate in the decade ahead. This is consistent with forecasts from the U.S. EIA in Figure 6-3.

As natural gas demand rises in the United States and abroad, U.S. prices that have been depressed for a number of years are likely to rise significantly.

CHAPTER 7

FUTURE ENERGY MIX

As the previous chapters in this section have shown, the future energy mix is changing. But it might not be in the way you think. Oil demand and natural gas demand are likely to rise sharply in the decade ahead, with China, India, emerging Asia, and other emerging markets at the epicenter of the surge in demand growth.

Meanwhile, the biggest sources of additional marginal supply for oil and natural gas are set to come from the United States, which has historically been a major net importer of hydrocarbons. This is a major changeup with economy, supply chain, and even national security ramifications. For a long time, the narrative in the United States has focused on rallying against foreign oil. And yet, now the United States is poised to export ever-increasing levels of crude oil, natural gas, and petroleum products.

Instead of putting the United States at a global disadvantage, it is now a bit more in the catbird seat, at a critical upstream point in the global economy just as Asia begins its full ascent.

Aside from the change-up of critical sources of additional marginal hydrocarbon supply and demand, the push against CO2 emissions and a push toward clean energy are likely to force a policy move away from coal across economies.

Coal consumption in the United States has been falling for a decade, while natural gas has been on the rise. At the same time, nuclear power has been relatively flat and renewables have been on the rise — especially renewables other than hydro, as can be seen in Figure 7-1. If the EIA projects are to be believed — and I think they are — this trend is likely to continue in the decade ahead and beyond. But while some things are expected to change, some will likely remain the same.

Figure 7-1: EIA U.S. Energy Consumption Mix Projections[1]

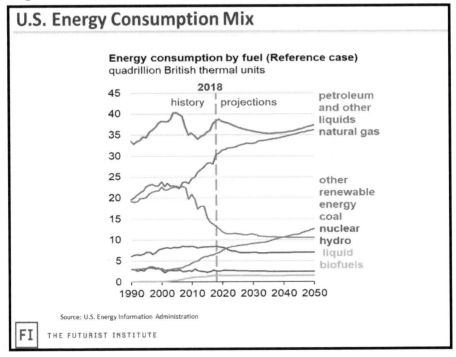

It is important to note that even if the U.S. energy mix — and especially the power mix — changes, petroleum fuels are expected to be the dominant form of energy consumed in the United States through 2050. Those are the official numbers. So for all the talk of electric vehicles, it is important to know that right now the outlook is still very oil-centric. And this is a function of the fact that there is no more efficient or more transportable form of energy than liquid hydrocarbons. This also means that energy demand will very much remain a mix in the United States and globally.

And the demand for oil, natural gas, and all other forms of energy is poised to rise globally in the decade ahead and beyond, as shown in the OPEC forecasts in Figure 7-2 and Figure 7-3.

Figure 7-2: Global Energy Demand by Fuel and Time[2]

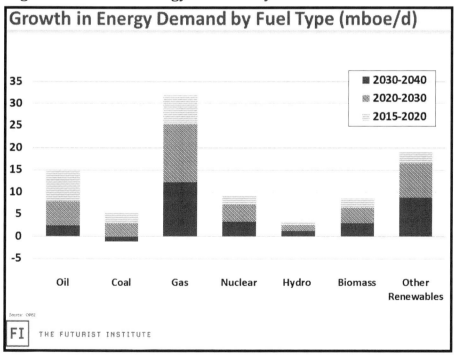

The emerging economies that will spur higher levels of oil consumption will also drive consumption of all kinds of energy sources. OPEC forecasts through 2050 also reflect expectations that demand globally will rise for all forms of energy.

Of course, it will vary greatly by region.

The wealthier OECD economies will make the biggest moves away from oil and coal to natural gas and renewables, but emerging economies will drive the lion's share of additional energy consumption in the decade ahead. And they will be consuming a lot more natural gas, a lot more oil, a lot more renewables, and a lot more coal.

Figure 7-3: Global Energy Growth by Type and Region[3]

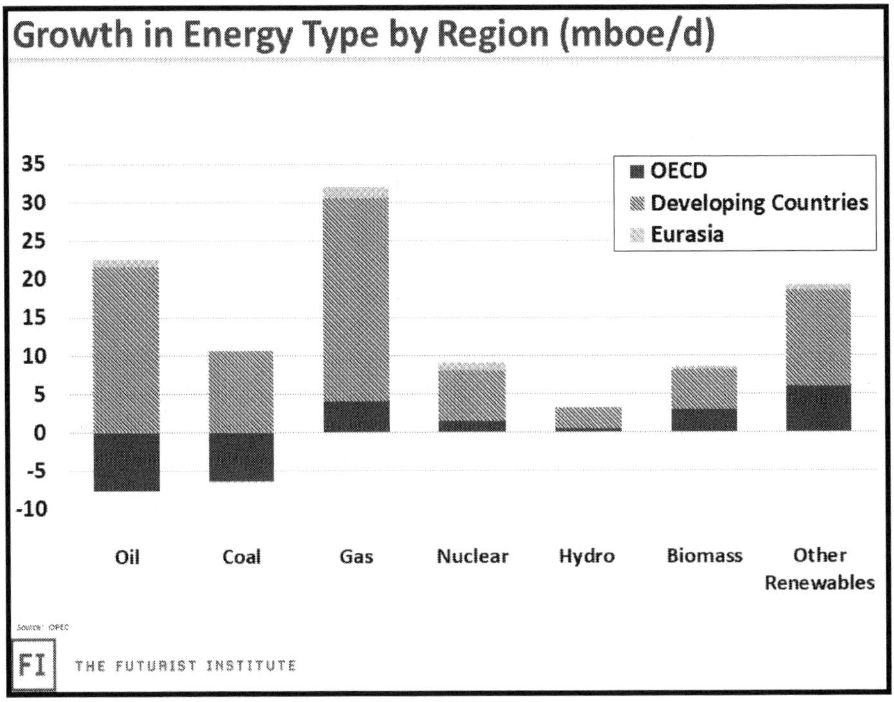

Growth in Energy Type by Region (mboe/d)

Source: OPEC

FI   THE FUTURIST INSTITUTE

Looking Ahead

Record levels of energy will be consumed in the decade ahead. There will be new record levels of consumption across energy classes set every year. Only coal risks having some down years, and even that may be a stretch, given the likely rise in emerging market demand for cheap power and the very low cost of coal on a nonexternality basis.

While the change in the global and U.S. energy consumption mix is likely to gain further traction and accelerate, this will largely remain a function of income and economic priorities that are often dictated by policies and encouraged with subsidies. This is why renewables have had greater success in Europe and why Europe will remain a flashpoint for further development.

In the United States, the only state with a viable chance to be net carbon zero in the coming decade is Hawaii, because of its exceptional geothermal, solar, and wind power assets. These are exceptional because they are dictated by natural topography that is incomparable elsewhere in the United States.

Of course, many people would love to live in economies purely fueled by renewables, but that is not likely to be a reality for very many places in the decade ahead. The costs are still too high, and there are also physical limitations.

So, for the foreseeable future, energy consumption is likely to rise — and be a mix of hydrocarbons and renewables.

Energy Demand-Side
Technologies

CHAPTER 8

ELECTRIC VEHICLES

Now we get to the part of the book that most people expected. For some readers, it may come as a surprise that this is Chapter 8, rather than Chapters 1-7. And this is where I have to splash some cold water on the topic.

There is a reason why the cover of this book is a mix of black and greens. Because the energy mix of the future will be just that — a mix. Crude oil, natural gas, and coal will remain critical elements of the energy mix. And power demand, which may be met with more hydrocarbon consumption, could rise farther with more electric vehicles on the road, even if the CO_2 implications are less negative with power generation on average than with petroleum fueled vehicles.

But the overarching truth is that the biggest jewel in the hype crown for the future of energy is the promise of electric vehicles.

Don't get me wrong! Like all other forms of energy, the demand for electric vehicles will rise significantly. But the imminent death of hydrocarbons has been wildly overhyped.

A lot of this has to do with what I call *hype locusts.*

This is an ever-increasing and all-too-common phenomenon where a technology topic becomes *en vogue,* and the media, social media, and then broader society extrapolate the emergence of this emerging new technology to assume it will instantly reach scale.

The assumption is that the problems are solved the minute any kind of technology is invented or first proven. And this causes a swarm of mindless attraction. Hence the term *hype locusts.*

As the hype locusts swarm, they can impact financial markets and private company funding rounds and valuations, and they can even impact political discourse and drive policy to impractical places. But there is immense danger in the foregone overextended teleological assumptions about a technology as *Deus ex machina* that can make resolving a major fundamental global problem into a simple *fait accompli.*

Unfortunately, this is roughly where we are with electric vehicles.

Adoption won't be overnight. And it is likely to be far from total.

To see the full scale of the hype, I would point you to the Google Trends graphs for both U.S. and global web searches for the terms "electric vehicles." As you can see in Figure 8-1, the U.S. search of this term is near highs not seen in almost a decade. In Figure 8-2, you can see that this term is near an all-time high on a global basis. But these figures show something else too.

Figure 8-1: Google Trends "EV" U.S. Web Search[1]

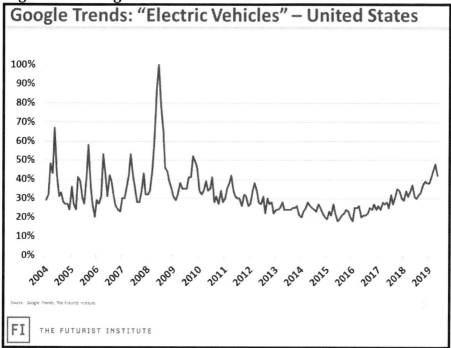

Figure 8-2: Google Trends "EV" Worldwide Web Search[2]

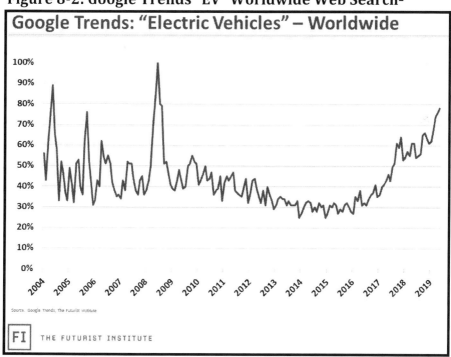

In both figures, you can see that the all-time high for the search term "electric vehicles" occurred during the middle of 2008, when oil prices hit their highest level in history. And that makes sense. Electric vehicles are generally more expensive than their conventional vehicle counterparts, so the total cost of ownership — or TCO, as supply chain and procurement professionals like to call it — would need to be a major purchasing-decision driver.

And the TCO of an electric vehicle makes the most financial sense and has the greatest ROI or potential for comparative ROI versus a conventional vehicle when fuel prices are at their highest. Ergo, the price of crude oil spiking to all-time highs engendered massive interest in electric vehicles because consumers were feeling the pinch of oil prices.

Now, however, oil prices are relatively low in the United States.

But fuel prices are perennially higher in Europe due to tax policies that can make fuel prices two to four times as expensive per gallon as in the United States. And there is a major policy focus on climate change in Europe. This is likely feeding the frenzy of interest in electric vehicles.

For U.S. readers, it is important to realize that oil and fuel prices are not just relatively cheap for U.S. consumers on a historical basis in 2019 compared to 2008, but that they are also cheaper on a comparative basis. This means that the adoption of electric vehicles could see a much greater push in Europe before there is such a push in the United States.

I first started covering both oil markets and the automotive sector in 2004 as the desk economist in the investment bank for the third-largest bank in the United States, Wachovia, which is now a part of Wells Fargo. As oil prices rose from 2004 through 2008, I frequently noted in my writings and in speeches thereafter that before everyone in the United States would switch to electric vehicles, there would be a switch to smaller cars, to more efficient cars, and to SUVs on car platforms rather than on truck chassis.

These incremental changes have since occurred, and miles-per-gallon rates have risen for vehicles. But the big takeaway here is that the changes, despite the high oil prices, were gradual and incremental.

And it really can't happen any other way.

The truth is that vehicle fleets take over a decade to turn over. And it's also important to know that consumer behavior can take time to change.

But more electric vehicles are certainly coming. And they are likely to come to the places with the highest fuel prices first. After all, the TCO benefits — the financial ROI — of owning an electric vehicle is still the primary driver of purchase decision.

Yes, there will be electric vehicle buyers who purchase because of a moral imperative or a desire to convey external value signaling, but corporate fleet purchases and most individual purchases will still come down to the cash.

You can see several forecasts for electric vehicle adoption in the next two figures. In Figure 8-3, you can see the U.S. EIA forecast of electric vehicle adoption.

This shows that even by 2050, electric vehicle adoption in the United States would represent only 10.7 percent of all vehicles in the fleet of cars and light trucks.

Even by 2050, this is still a small percentage. In absolute terms, the EIA is predicting that there would be over 31 million electric light vehicles on the road in the United States by 2050. But the total of light vehicles it forecasts will be on the road is close to 295 million vehicles.

Figure 8-3: U.S. EIA Forecast of Electric Vehicles in Fleet[3]

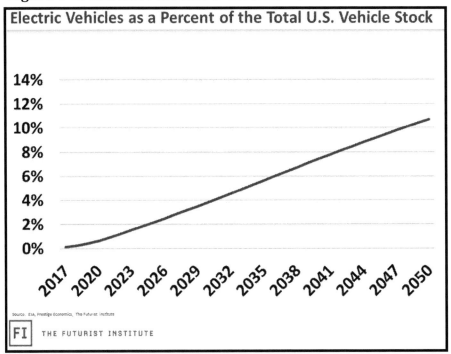

OPEC has a more aggressive global reference case than the EIA for global light electric vehicle market penetration of 15.3 percent by 2040.[4] This is a lot greater than the U.S. EIA forecast of a light vehicle fleet penetration for electric vehicles of only 7.4 percent. The more aggressive OPEC forecast could be accounted for, in part, by a likely greater adoption of electric vehicles in Europe, where fuels are taxed heavily, as I noted above.

The more rapid global adoption of electric vehicles also means that an extrapolated 2050 electric vehicle global fleet stock penetration number could be between 20 and 25 percent. That's a lot stronger than the EIA forecasts for the United States. It is also important to note that OPEC's forecast expectations show a much slower adoption rate, despite high utilization rates.

Figure 8-4: OPEC Forecast of Electric Vehicles in Fleet[5]

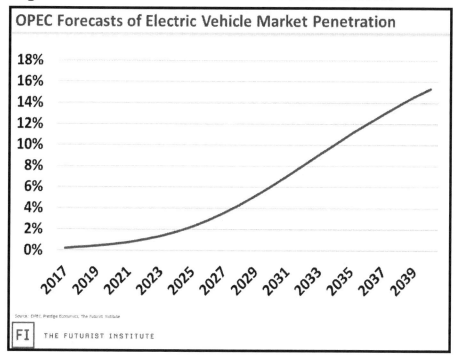

OPEC's forecasts reflect an expectation that only 4 percent of the global commercial vehicle fleet will be electric by 2040.[6]

But despite relatively slow adoption paces of purely electric vehicles, the adoption of other alternative vehicles, including ethanol, biofuel, natural gas, propane, fuel cell, and hybrids, is also likely to rise.

And more electric vehicles will certainly be purchased, especially as the technology for the vehicles makes them cheaper to manufacture. But the truth is that while much of the technology in electric vehicles can be driven down by at-scale levels of production and additional R&D, one of the biggest sticking points will remain battery costs.

Commodity prices don't go down if the commodities in question are of limited supply and the market is seeing a massive rise in global demand.

This is one of the reasons hedge funds and corporations have rushed to secure their supply chains of critical electric vehicle battery elements, like cobalt and lithium. Although these prices fell during 2018, along with many other metals prices, they still remained high in absolute terms. Lithium average annual prices even saw an all-time high for the total year of 2018. You can see the trend of cobalt prices in Figure 8-5 and lithium prices in Figure 8-6.

In a 2015 interview, Bill Gates even noted that "we need an energy miracle."[7]

To this end, Gates founded Breakthrough Energy Ventures as a $1 billion innovation fund, which is now also supported and funded by a slew of other billionaires, including Jeff Bezos, Richard Branson, Michael Bloomberg, and Jack Ma.[8]

The reason this fund is important for our discussion of electric vehicles is that limited supplies of cobalt and lithium present real physical issues in terms of electric vehicle fleet penetration.

And one of the companies that Gates' fund has backed is KoBald Metals. It is a company that uses "Machine Prospector technology [to combine] never-before-used datasets with conventional geochemical, geophysical, and geological data in statistical association models to identify prospects ."[9]

Figure 8-5: Cobalt Prices[10]

In other words, there is a company in Gates' portfolio scouring the earth's crust for more cobalt deposits — for that energy miracle. These supplies are so coveted that Apple secured cobalt directly from miners in 2018.[11]

And Apple makes phones and laptops — not cars.

So, if Apple is worried about having enough cobalt to make the batteries for its phones, iPads, and computers, you better believe that companies like Tesla should be on top of this risk. Because this is the potential make-or-break factor for electric vehicles.

Of course, some are forecasting declines in electric vehicle battery costs, but we are skeptical.

Figure 8-6: Lithium Prices[12]

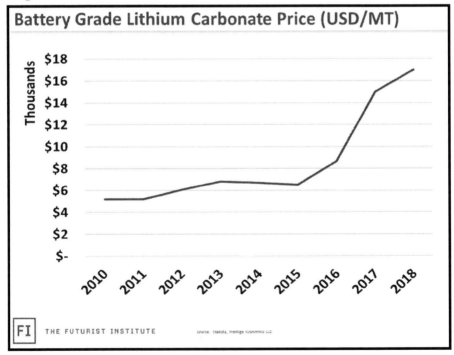

Figure 8-7 shows data from a recent Bloomberg article on electric vehicle battery costs based on data from Bloomberg NEF.

But as I noted already in this chapter, there is a different between lower costs of manufacturing from improved R&D, technology, and at-scale operations. However, commodity prices don't go down if the commodities in question are of limited supply and the market is seeing a massive rise in global demand.

Aside from the questions of commodity supplies for batteries, there is also a question of efficacy when it comes to reducing CO_2 emissions. If that's the goal with electric vehicles, it is not always the case.

Figure 8-7: Forecast of Battery Cost for Electric Vehicles[13]

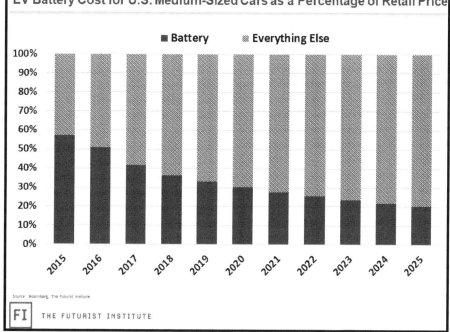

Bill Gates noted back in November 2015 that when people are worried about CO2, they often assume electric vehicles will make the situation better. He noted:

> People think, *Oh, well, I'll just get an electric car.* There are places where if you buy an electric car, you're actually increasing CO2 emissions, because the electricity infrastructure is emitting more CO2 than you would have if you'd had a gasoline powered car.[14]

Although this has been hotly debated, U.S. EIA data reflect that electric vehicles have lower emissions than conventional vehicles both nationally — and in all 50 states. The national average can be seen in Figure 8-8.

Figure 8-8: Average CO2 Emissions per U.S. Vehicle[15]

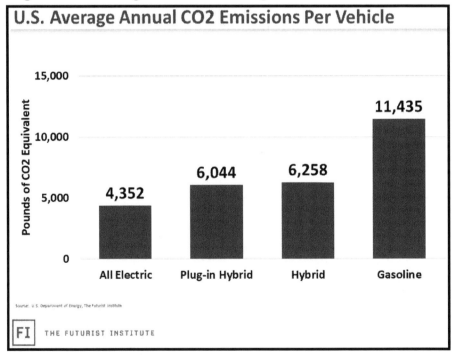

Looking Ahead

Electric vehicles will have an important role to play in the future of transportation and the future of energy. But that role in the coming decade and beyond is likely to still be relatively small compared to vehicles that consume petroleum fuels.

This may be disappointing, but it is based on the economic, physical, and chemistry-linked reality that liquid hydrocarbons are the cheapest, most efficient, transportable form of energy that currently exists on earth. And consumers will make decisions based on the economics of their purchases.

Essentially, oil prices are far too cheap to induce mass vehicle fleet conversion over to electric vehicles. And even if oil prices were markedly higher, there would still be real physical limitations when it comes to batteries.

After all, water may be roughly two-thirds of the planet, and oil is nowhere near as abundant as water. But the metals that go into electric vehicle batteries are scarcer still.

Electric vehicles are the hottest topic when talking about the future of energy. But the economic realities and physical limitations cannot be ignored. Without an energy miracle in the form of a battery technology step change and/or miraculous discoveries of massive and cheap lithium and cobalt deposits, the pace of adoption and total fleet penetration of electric vehicles is likely to remain quite low for the foreseeable future.

CHAPTER 9

E-COMMERCE

The self-service revolution is real.

E-commerce is the name of that revolution.

And additional energy demand will be a major consequence.

As we think about the future of energy, one topic that is perhaps more important than electric vehicles but gets overlooked is e-commerce.

This isn't a change of technology for petroleum fuel use abatement or increased efficiency. In fact, it is almost entirely the opposite.

E-commerce is experiencing massive growth, and it is a growing part of the supply chain that operates in the background. And it is being driven by fundamental consumer demand, which is nothing short of an unstoppable force, especially in the United States, where consumption is almost 70 percent of the U.S. economy.

The U.S. supply chain was not set up for single-piece batching. It was designed for palettes of goods to be sent to retail locations, and individuals would go to those retail stores and acquire many different goods. This is in many ways much more efficient than ordering individual goods at will online that get delivered to you throughout the day. This is why e-commerce is something that is likely to inadvertently drive up energy demand in a significant way in the decade ahead.

Also, regardless of how you may view the expectations for electric vehicles that I described in the preceding chapter, the likely continued future rise of e-commerce is also something that we are unlikely to disagree about.

Figure 9-1: U.S. E-Commerce in Dollar Terms[1]

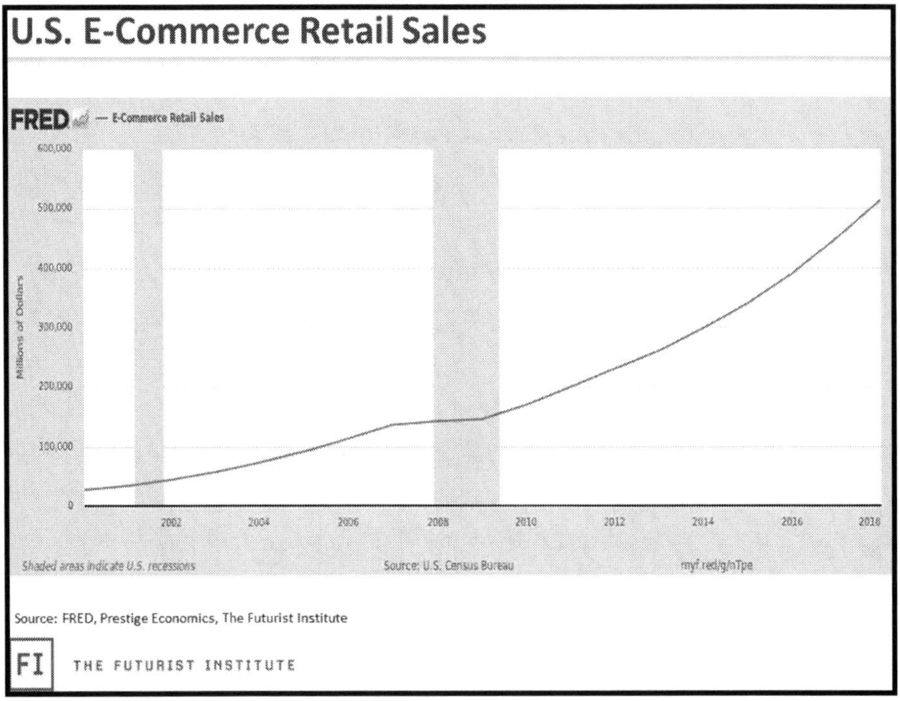

Source: FRED, Prestige Economics, The Futurist Institute

At an annual level of just $27 billion in 2000, e-commerce retail sales in the United States was worth $513 billion in 2018. This can be seen in Figure 9-1. And the trend shows no sign of stopping, let alone slowing.

Furthermore, this isn't just an inflation phenomenon. The percent of e-commerce has also been rising during that time period. At less than 1 percent of retail in Q1 2000, it was just shy of 10 percent of all U.S. retail sales in Q4 2018. This quarterly data and the steady trendline higher in percent of retail sales can be seen in Figure 9-2.

With a continued rise in e-commerce retail sales in absolute and percent of total terms, energy demand is likely to rise as well.

Figure 9-2: U.S. E-Commerce as a Percent of All Retail Sales[2]

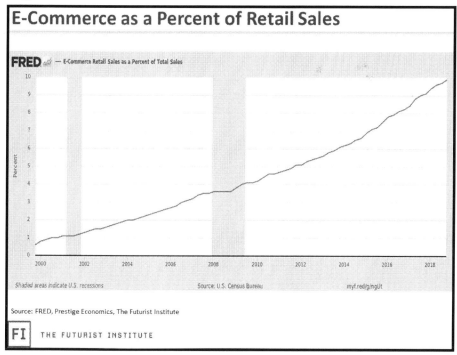

We at Prestige Economics expect that the percent of retail sales from e-commerce will rise over the coming decade, being around 25 percent by 2030. That's a massive increase. And it will put significant strains on the U.S. supply chain and will massively drive up the need for transportation and customized distribution.

The consequence is likely to be seen in U.S. miles driven. In 2018, miles driven was at a record level of over 3.2 trillion miles. This can be seen in Figure 9-3. We expect that number of miles to rise as e-commerce expands further, especially into food and grocery delivery, which have historically been more difficult areas for e-commerce vendors to penetrate. Only with highly efficient use of big data will e-commerce companies be able to mitigate runaway transportation and fuel demand.

Figure 9-3: U.S. Miles Driven[3]

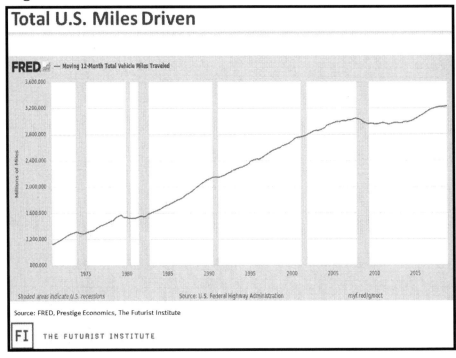

Source: FRED, Prestige Economics, The Futurist Institute

Looking Ahead

The rise of e-commerce, with associated fuel demands, isn't just going to be a domestic phenomenon or risk. Global e-commerce has expanded significantly, and it is expected to expand farther as well. As with the U.S. economy, the supply chains of other nations were not designed to handle single-piece batching.

In Figure 9-4, you can see that e-commerce represented 11.9 percent of global retail sales in 2018. Statista predicts it will represent 17.5 percent of global retail sales by 2021. We at Prestige Economics expect global e-commerce will be close to 25 percent of total global retail sales by 2030. Even if companies can leverage data to be as efficient as possible, this will significantly drive up global transportation fuel demand.

Figure 9-4: Global E-Commerce as Percent of Retail[4]

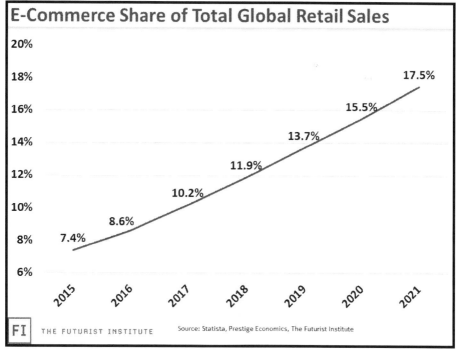

CHAPTER 10

TELECOMMUTING

While e-commerce presents upside demand for energy in the decade ahead, the trend of telecommuting presents the opportunity for some potential limits on increases in fuel demand — and in some regions it may present the opportunity for a reduction in some consumer transportation fuel demand.

Put simply, telecommuting is working from home.

From an energy standpoint, if you don't have to leave your home to go to work, you don't need to drive and you don't need to have two spaces — your home and your office — cooled or heated to account for climate control.

As you can see in Figure 10-1, telecommuting as a means of getting to work increased the most between 2005 and 2015. This growth in the telecommuting sector was already emerging in the mid-2000s, and it is a subject I discussed in my book *Jobs for Robots*.

The value propositions for increased telecommuting are simple.

Aside from saving time for workers, it also saves costs for employers. Employers do not need to spend as much on commercial office space or on parking spaces if workers never come into an office.

Plus, reliability is also arguably higher when people telecommute. Everyone that has ever worked for me at Prestige Economics, which I founded in 2009, has telecommuted. We don't have an office because we don't need one. All I care about is that people complete their tasks correctly and on time.

Figure 10-1: The Rise of Telecommuting[1]

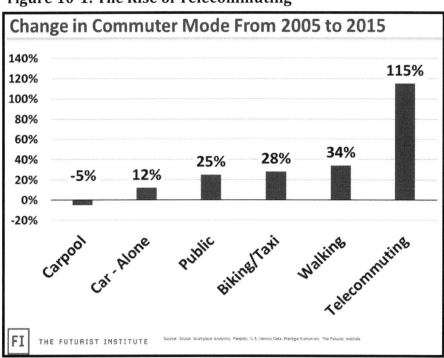

Looking Ahead

Telecommuting will continue to rise in the decade ahead. This is especially true in developed economies, where climate change and environmental targets can be more easily met by lowering the number of people who drive to work or operate out of the office. Plus, the percentage of telecommuters with a bachelor's or graduate degree is greater than for non-telecommuters, as you can see in Figure 10-2. This means that as we continue to move toward more intellectual-capital-focused economies, we will see more opportunities for telecommuting. This isn't going to be a dynamic that stems the tide of rising energy and fuel demand due to significant expansions in the global population and emerging market global wealth. But telecommuting is a trend we will see more frequently in the decade ahead.

Figure 10-2: Education Levels of Telecommuters[2]

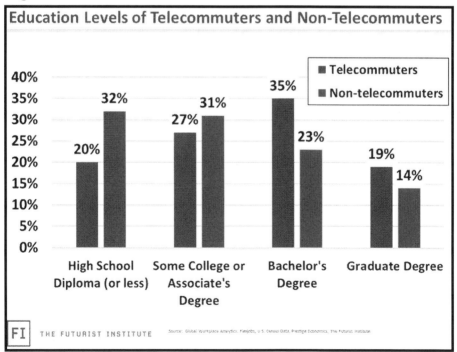

CHAPTER 11

SMART POWER

The biggest challenge in the world of power is how to most efficiently operate the power assets you have at your disposal. This is driven by a few factors, but most importantly, supply responds to demand, and there are two kinds of power demand, generally. First, there is on-peak demand, which usually occurs during the waking hours of the day, when people are up doing things and consuming power. Second, there is off-peak power demand, which generally occurs at night, when people are asleep and not consuming much power.

For a very long time, the only relationship power companies had with their customers was a one-way relationship, in which power was provided and the utility company often had to struggle to estimate load in advance. In recent years, however, many homes have been outfitted with smart meters. This has arguably been the biggest change of the past decade for power transmission and load serving. Essentially, smart meters feed information back into the grid, back to power providers, which helps improve power load dispatching, load serving, and power asset use.

According to the EIA, "by the end of 2016, U.S. electric utilities had installed about 71 million advanced metering infrastructure (AMI) smart meters, covering 47% of the 150 million electricity customers in the United States."[1] This dynamic can be seen in Figure 11-1, where you can see the percentage of U.S. customers with smart meters by 2016. And it can also be seen in Figure 11-2, where you can see the number of U.S. customers with smart meters by the end of 2016.

The value of smart meters is that they provide two-way feedback and communication between power consumers and providers. These meters use "real-time or near real-time electricity data."[2] In addition to providing information about demand and pricing, smart meters can also provide information about outages.

Figure 11-1: Percent of U.S. Customers With Smart Meters[3]

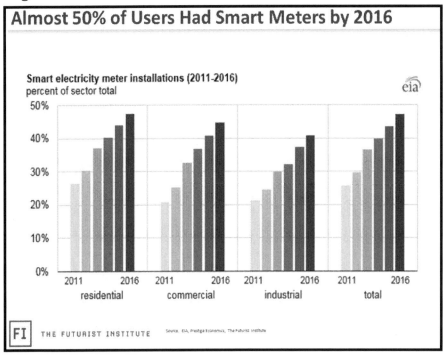

The rollout of smart meters is also expanding globally as well. For example, E.U. countries have committed to "rolling out close to 200 million smart meters for electricity and 45 million for gas by 2020...[when] it is expected that almost 72% of European consumers will have a smart meter for electricity while 40% will have one for gas."[4]

Looking Ahead

Smart meters will be rolled out in more and more regions and countries because they add value. They help create data that can improve efficiency, improve reliability, reduce cost, reduce waste, and help power providers make more informed decisions to meet corporate, environmental, or other goals.

Figure 11-2: U.S. Customers With Smart Meters[5]

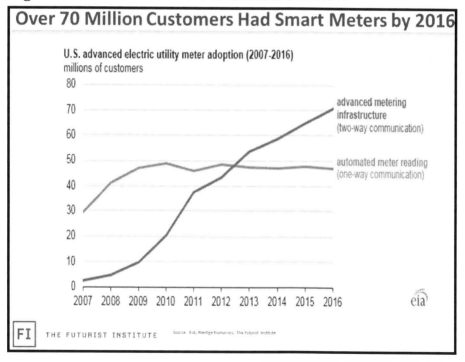

Energy Supply-Side Data Technologies

CHAPTER 12

USING DATA TO UNLOCK VALUE

There is tremendous value in data. But you need to know how to unlock that value.

This is the theme of my book *The Fog of Data.*

The importance of data is also something I mentioned in two of the past three chapters. You see, data will play a critical role in managing the demands of e-commerce to optimally dispatch individual batch orders as e-commerce more than doubles as a percent of retail sales in the decade ahead.

Meanwhile, data will also be critical for optimizing power dispatch in smart grids. Here, data also present another opportunity to improve energy efficiency.

But beyond the hope that data will help fulfill the promise of e-commerce and maximize the benefits of smart meters, there is also the hope that data can also help optimize how other companies in the energy supply chain operate.

Data collection, analysis, and use will have value is in a few different ways. First, is the concept of **predictive analytics**. The idea here is that by collecting a lot of data, trends may emerge that allow you to be able to make predictions of future use and behavior. This could be just as critical for real-time power dispatch as it is for the dispatch of physical e-commerce orders from a mobile distribution center.

Essentially, predictive analytics is based on statistical analyses, as is most work in the field of data. The most important point here is that it is important to collect data that drives at the question you fundamentally want answered. It is also important that you follow a consistent and stable data process of collection, cleaning, and preparing your data. I have discussed this at length in several of my books, so I will just share Figure 12-1 as an illustration.

Following a data process is important whether you are doing predictive analytics or whether you are trying to create machine-learning algorithms. **Machine learning** is the next area of unlocking data value that we should discuss.

If predictive analytics is forecasting and statistics, then machine learning is using data to help identify patterns. It can be as simple as conditional Boolean statements layered on top of each other as a sort of nested set of conditional statements.

For example, if I like doughnuts and croissants, a machine learning algorithm may deduce that I would like a cronut, which is a combination of the two. This is a very simplified example, but you can imagine how the conditional statements might look.

If donut = like and croissant = like, then cronut = recommend.

As I noted above, some people may just call this an algorithm, where a pattern is identified. And it can be based on some statistical analysis of massive panel data. This could be true for drilling for oil and gas just as much as for recommending cronuts to me. The conditions might be looking for patterns of what preconditions are necessary for drilling a good oil well.

Plus, machine learning can also be done with physical machines — not just with data analysis to draw statistically likely conclusions or make probable recommendations. In that respect, it can be a form of limited hardware automation too.

Figure 12-1: Follow a Data Process

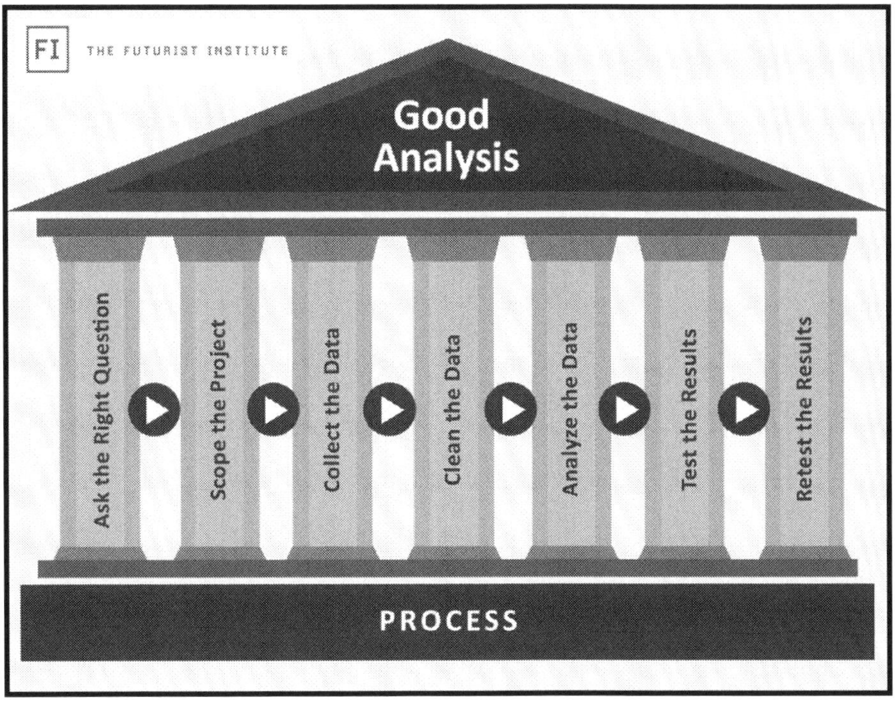

Although people like to throw around the words *machine learning* and *artificial intelligence*, we are still a bit farther away from a true form of **artificial intelligence, or AI**. I will discuss this more in the next chapter, because while AI is limited now, we are likely to see more use of large sets of data to derive potential implications with predictive analytics (to make predictions) and machine learning (to use statistics and conditional programming to identify patterns and make predictions). And we are also likely to see a greater use of AI and quantum computing (or at least emulated quantum computing) to support AI that seeks out and identifies patterns independently with ever-diminished levels of human guidance and inputs.

Looking Ahead

As in other sectors, companies throughout the energy world — in the oil patch as well as renewables and electric vehicles — will need to find ways to optimize their activities and to automate what they can. Only by analyzing data will companies be able to become more efficient in their processes and automate their activities by codifying and more rapidly perform tasks to demonstrate and achieve significant efficiency gains.

Only by analyzing data — lots of data — will energy companies be able to boost their productivity and profitability. With better data analysis, energy companies can make the molecules go farther, they can make drilling more efficient, they can take cost out of their operations, and they could improve the battery technology on which many hopes about the future of energy hinge.

CHAPTER 13

QUANTUM COMPUTING

Last year, I wrote a book called *Quantum: Computing Nouveau*, which explored the nature of quantum computing as a new kind of computation that is likely to make big strides in the decade ahead. Unlike your normal computer today, quantum computers use quantum bits, or qubits, rather than regular (i.e., binary) bits.

There is additional processing power in qubits compared to bits, and it is a bit complicated to explain, but basically qubits can exist in three positions rather than just two. Also, qubits have their highest value use in solving problems with large sets of data by performing probabilistic, non-deterministic calculations to provide the most likely solution to what could be a very odd or complicated question.

Energy was one of the six areas that I examined for potential quantum computing use cases, along with finance, government, healthcare, transport & logistics, and agriculture.

In Figure 13-1, you can see how I assessed the potential impact and potential implementation of quantum computing in the world of energy.

Regardless of energy sector, we found the highest-value use cases for quantum computing to be in risk trading and hedging as well as in energy arbitrage trading. The reason behind the trading value proposition is that there is a massive amount of data, and while there are already algorithms in place to analyze and optimize energy trading and hedging, a more efficient, effective, and accurate model would always be preferred.

In other words, quantum computing may be a better answer.

Figure 13-1: Energy and Quantum Computing

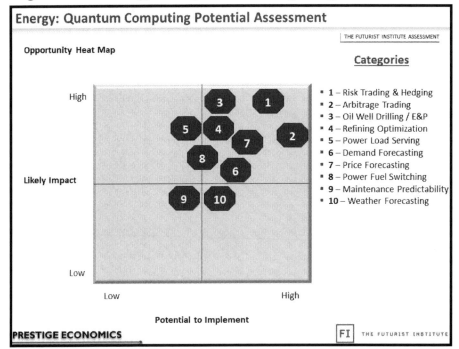

One of the areas where energy demand and price forecasting may overlap operationally would be in oil refining, where the use of quantum computing could optimize operations. The industry has long run on linear program models, but perhaps quantum computing may offer quicker, slightly more optimized, and more valuable solutions. A rough equivalent of oil-refining optimization in the power space would be optimal load serving and power fuel switching (between coal, gas, and renewables).

Similar to the trading value propositions of quantum computing in oil and gas would also be the potential use cases for forecasting commodity prices, demand, and weather. These are important factors that impact operations and corporate profits. And they are driven by inputs across massive data sets.

In the field of oil and gas, there is also a high-value potential use case in analyzing seismic data for drilling oil and gas wells. The data sets are massive, and the search to drill the perfect well in the perfect rocks is a wildcatter's dream — as well as the dream of independent oil majors and NOCs alike.

One final area for consideration in oil and gas is maintenance predictability. Although this may not be as exciting as fuel switching, arbitrage trading, or wildcatting, there could be significant corporate value in using quantum to create more effective predictive maintenance programs at energy facilities. This is likely to be less impactful than some of the areas I've discussed. But it is still likely in the running to use quantum computing.

Looking Ahead

Quantum computing will eventually be very important for energy. But the overall impact it might have in the next decade could be a bit more limited due to the timeline of quantum development and the physical and material science limitations associated with quantum technology, especially traditional quantum computers that exist as steampunk chandeliers kept inside refrigeration units at near absolute zero temperatures that are cooled by liquid nitrogen to limit decoherence during computational processing.

In any case, quantum is likely to make big strides in the decade ahead, despite the physical limitations and material science issues that could prevent a traditional universal quantum computer from achieving full commercial viability.

Of course, a full level of universal quantum could support a more complete form of AI. But even if quantum computing does not reach full viability in the next decade, emulated quantum computing could boost processing power. And even if quantum developments are slow, they will impact cybersecurity planning and requirements so that encryptions can last into a quantum computing era. And with or without quantum, more advanced AI is still coming. The question is what kind of — and how many — processors it will take to get there.

For oil and gas, power, renewables, and other energy clean tech, more computational power should help companies and economies better harness the power of energy they use to maximize efficiency and make each molecule go farther in the decade ahead.

CHAPTER 14

BLOCKCHAIN

Blockchain is one of the tech world's greatest Zeitgeisty buzzwords. In fact, I wrote the book *The Promise of Blockchain* to help put the discussion of blockchain in a context for discourse.

The well-known frenzied rise of cryptocurrencies isn't the only part of the blockchain world. In fact, even though blockchain is the technology that underpins cryptocurrencies, it can be used for so much more.

In essence, blockchain technology is a kind of multiparty verification system, accounting database, and permanent record.

It can allow multiple parties to share a distributed record — a ledger — of transactions that is permanent. And within a trusted network of counterparties, this distributed record could prove extremely valuable for record-keeping activities like tracing physical goods to their origins and destinations or demonstrating local content use, which is often required of IOCs operating in a foreign country or under the direction of an NOC.

To recap, blockchain is a kind of accounting database and record-keeping system with special permissions and multiple party access.

As a futurist, I believe it is important to place technological developments in a historical context. And blockchain is just one of the newest of many recordkeeping database technologies.

And it is highly unlikely to be the last.

For now, blockchain technology offers the hope and promise of distributed information and knowledge that can reduce costs, add economic value, and prevent a Library of Alexandria-level loss of information and institutional knowledge for corporate, governmental, and private entities.

For oil and gas, as in other commodity businesses, blockchain offers a lot of benefits in terms of transparency. I understand it seems ironic that something used as the basis of anonymous and trustless cryptocurrency transactions is also the foundation of full supply chain transparency, but that's the deal.

Hopefully, now it is a bit clearer why blockchain itself, as a technology, has a tremendous corporate value proposition. Companies are exposed to central points of failure, and blockchain technology could reduce those risks by sharing information across a distributed network. But this is not without risks, as it would increase the attack surface of the entity using the blockchain, which is a critical issue for cybersecurity.

In Figure 14-1, I have included The Futurist Institute's assessment of blockchain potential in the areas of transport and logistics. Since energy is a physical business that requires physical movements of goods, this is an important graphic.

The nine areas of high-potential use cases in transportation and logistics are as follows:

Freight Tracking   **Trade Customs & Duties**
Chain of Custody   **Conflict Minerals**
Local Content   **Restricted Chemicals**
Restricted Agriculture   **Pharma Tracking**
Intellectual Property

Figure 14-1: Blockchain Potential in Transportation

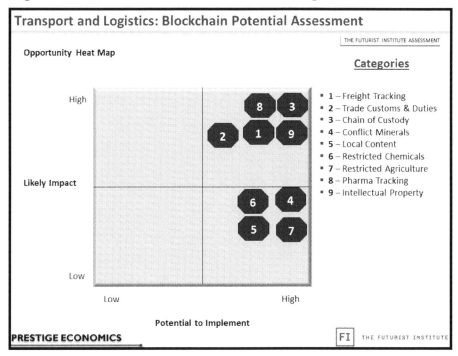

Looking Ahead

With so many potential uses for blockchain in the energy supply chain, we are likely to see broad-based adoption and use at some levels. Again, we would expect this for its record-keeping value, whether it be to demonstrate local content, better track chains of custody, or have more easily auditable records.

While there are several ways that blockchain technology could be adopted in the oil patch, one area where energy is likely to shy away from blockchain is with cryptocurrencies. The crypto fad showed massive levels of profitability, but it led to the biggest financial bubble in history while simultaneously being hijacked by nefarious market participants and political bad actors to engage in election tampering, terrorist activities, money laundering, and all kinds of other mobster stuff.

A corporatized digital payment system that works within banking regulatory frameworks and systems could be palatable to the energy industry, however. But it would need to be used for B2B or even bank-to-bank transactions in a way that increases the speed of payment processing. That kind of crypto could be well received in the oil patch — as in all industries. And we are going to see more of these.

But any kind of digital payment system or quasi-cryptocurrency would be more likely to have pegged values that are linked to a specific currency. And they are more likely to be highly regulated. In that way, they would be fully above board in terms of their use cases — and they would embody minimal risk levels.

For oil and gas, fast payment processing could be a godsend because some companies often operate in emerging markets where banking and financial systems can be a bit more dodgy — or at least they suffer from slower payment terms, compared to the terms and clearing in more established OECD economies.

For this reason, more rapid cross-border digital payments in a clear and clean legal, regulated environment could prove attractive in the decade ahead. A blockchain-based digital payment system that accelerates the velocity of money and improves payment terms without adding minimal risk is likely to gain traction along with the multiparty verification, database, and recordkeeping blockchain accounting use case.

Energy Supply-Side Physical Technologies

CHAPTER 15

AUTOMATION

One of the biggest changes that will come to energy in the decade ahead is automation. You will see this in the energy patch, at rigs and oil pads, in power plants, and at R&D facilities for clean technology.

Automation will be everywhere. But this doesn't mean it will make all the energy jobs go away. In fact, it could be far from it!

The best way to think of automation is as an extension of delegation. Automation can help individuals and organizations build leverage to get more work done with fewer or the same number of people. Essentially, it's a productivity lever.

The move to automation is occurring across industries, and energy is going to be taken along for the ride of robots, chatbots, software scripts, and other forms of automation. The best and highest use of automation and technology is to perform tasks that are unpleasant, repetitive, predictable, and dangerous. And companies need to find as many ways as possible to do this.

The reason this is so important to consider is that the workforce is aging. And in the current low unemployment environment there is a savagely fierce war on talent that is affecting energy companies, technology companies, and every other kind of company in the United States.

Demographic shifts in other OECD economies are even more pronounced. The average European is about 10 years older than the average American. And the birthrates are sharply lower in other OECD countries than in the United States.

In the end, the decision to automate will be quite simple.

Every dollar you spend on technology that automates a process that is unsafe, unpleasant, or repetitive frees up worker time and adds productivity. The ROI calculation on these kinds of expenses should be the value of your time freed up compared to the cost of the automated solution.

There are two levels of automation that are important to consider, and they fall into a futurist framework that I discuss often: **almost now** versus **maybe someday**.

An example of *almost now* automation would be assistance at well sites with automated vehicles transporting equipment.

An example of *maybe someday* automation would be humanoid-type robots running pipe down hole in a drilling process. In other words, actual robot roughnecks are still a ways out.

In the following chapter, I will discuss in more detail some of the expectations I have for physical energy operations and automation in the coming decade. But a lot of those concepts are tied to physical operations and include maintenance of pipelines in remote or dangerous areas as well as transporting physical equipment using automated vehicles.

But these are not the only kinds of automation that energy will be using. It's important to realize that predictive and repetitive tasks in the office will be automated as well, especially mid-office and back-office activities. At first, these solutions will work with people to augment human capital, but over time you'll see more comprehensive automation.

Looking Ahead

Automation is coming to the world of energy, in all its forms. Because reducing cost is the number one area companies see value, they will use technology to augment headcount and drive up productivity, but they will also use automation to limit production costs and purchasing costs as a way to maximize profits. Plus, since some energy-related jobs are dangerous, more automation is likely to be used to improve safety — and lower insurance premiums.

One thing is certain: Energy companies of the future need to be technology companies at their core. And technology companies will be focused on automation as an extension of delegation. Ergo, energy companies will be rolling out automation solutions in the decade ahead.

CHAPTER 16

OPERATIONAL DRONES

At the time this book went to print, most people thought of flying drones as toys with entertainment or kitsch value. You know, something you might buy at Brookstone as a holiday gift.

But for energy supply chain purposes, the greatest future kind of drone isn't going to be 12 inches wide and carry a digital camera around as it follows you to record every second of your next European vacation for posterity on Instagram and Snapchat.

Of course, those kinds of drones will grow in use as well.

But those aren't the kinds of drones that will significantly impact the energy business. A better comparison for drones that will have big economic impact would be flying military drones that are adapted to have a dual use purpose for transporting industrial equipment to remote locations. These will be critical for monitoring oil and gas assets, as well as repairing, supplying, and supporting remote oil and gas activities.

Oil and gas companies that operate in remote regions of the world will likely find high value in these kinds of flying industrial transport drones, which could fly in pipes, drilling equipment, refinery parts, and other major equipment to remote areas, where roads are insufficient or nonexistent.

These kinds of drones could be used for all kinds of oil and gas construction projects, as well as building power plants and other energy-related facilities. Instead of building structures and then transporting them piecemeal to extremely remote areas for assembly, the parts could be transported by drones with wingspans of five or 10 meters — or even more. And eventually, they could be assembled, repaired, or replaced without human interactions.

This isn't just a maybe, by the way. Some of the companies I work with are actively exploring these options for supporting their oil and gas drilling activities. The challenges of infrastructure have been particularly acute in regions when the oil and gas industry booms and roads can't handle the traffic. Drones could overcome that challenge. As the quote from the movie *Back to the Future* goes, "Where we're going, we don't need roads."

And energy industry drones won't just be in the skies.

For oil and gas, autonomous vehicles will also be underwater — and on the roads. And they will increasingly support operations in dangerous environments, where there are high environmental, safety, or K&R risks.

Underwater drones are already in development and deployment. Given that subsea pipelines have been mapped in the North Sea and the U.S. Gulf Coast, this gives the autonomous subsea vehicles a map to work off of.

Wheeled vehicles are coming, too. After all, on-road autonomous vehicles have already reached minimum viable product. So, it makes plenty of sense that warehouse-like autonomous vehicles or robots (in the R2-D2 sense of boxes on wheels, rather than the C-3PO humanoid sense) are likely to come to support operations in somewhat controlled environments like refineries or oil and gas pads.

Looking Ahead

Over the coming decade, drones and other kinds of autonomous vehicles will become an increasingly critical part of the energy industry. But as with other disruptive supply chain technologies ahead, there will be challenges for drones. One of the biggest risks will be that drones may be hackable and that regulations may prohibit industrial and retail last mile drone development. This is especially a risk if roads and skies become very crowded with drones that appear to be everywhere.

Flying drones and subsea drones are likely to have a material impact in extending the reach of global energy supply chains by increasing access to regions, assets, and markets that were previously exceptionally isolated. It also means that throughout the entire energy supply chain, autonomy will become a critical lever of productivity. And autonomous vehicles will also be a critical element that increases safety and operational reliability.

Trends in Clean Energy and Renewables

CHAPTER 17

CLEAN POWER

As with electric vehicle batteries, many people are hopeful about the prospects for renewable energy. But while electric vehicles are the jewel in the crown of hype in the future of energy, renewable power is viewed much more realistically. The hope and likely reality of more renewable power is clear.

The push toward clean power will continue, especially as the focus on climate change increases. Even now, at the time of writing this book, the term "climate change" showed record high levels in web searches conducted in the United States and near record-high levels worldwide. These dynamics can be seen in Figures 17-1 and 17-2, respectively.

But despite the rising concern, discourse, and interest in climate change, there are critical fundamental limitations.

The truth is that hydrocarbons are wildly cheap and efficient. It will be truly difficult to enact global moves away from CO_2 and toward clean energy as long as oil and gas and coal are super cheap, which they are.

This is especially true on an economic multiplier basis, because energy isn't just a luxury good people buy once they become middle class. Energy in all its forms is a fundamental ingredient and driver of economic growth. And a lack of access to power is a key metric of global poverty.

If economies and societies decide they want to move away from hydrocarbons, then taxes will need to rise, and subsidies will need to be enacted or increased for renewables. But since energy is an economic multiplier, some economic growth will be lost in the process. And the political will it would require may exceed that of politicians in countries outside Western Europe, where CO_2 and high fuel taxes have already been implemented to incentivize certain behaviors that reduce E.U. emissions.

Figure 17-1: U.S. Climate Change Web Searches[1]

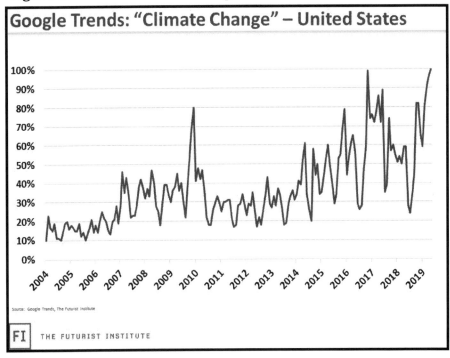

Looking Ahead

The need for significant political will to enact change in the United States should be clear even if we just consider vehicle fuel prices. After all, U.S. fuel prices are 50 percent to 75 percent cheaper than they are in Europe. Want to find out how much political will it takes to encourage renewables and green energy? Try raising the U.S. gasoline tax.

For the record, this is not my recommendation. Please don't send me hate mail. I merely wish to illustrate what it would take to enact significant changes, and I think most people intuitively realize that politicians and their constituents may not be willing to pay the true price for the externalities, as economists call it, that come with the energy we consume.

Figure 17-2: Worldwide Climate Change Web Searches[2]

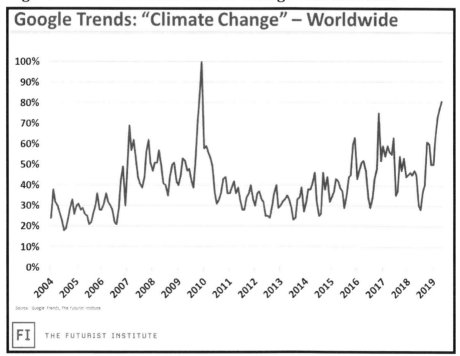

Another major challenge ahead for CO2 is that even if OECD economies reduce their output, the global level of emissions is poised to rise in coming years, because global energy demand is rising. In fact, the EIA forecasts that growth in emissions is likely to continue in 2019, which can be seen below in Figure 17-3.

Although the pace of emissions growth has slowed in recent years, the trend has still been higher. And rising global energy demands will prevent a challenge for limiting CO2 production on a global basis. This means that even with the political will and effort of OECD economies, it may not be enough to significantly reduce annual global CO2 emissions in the coming decade.

Figure 17-3: Global Emissions[3]

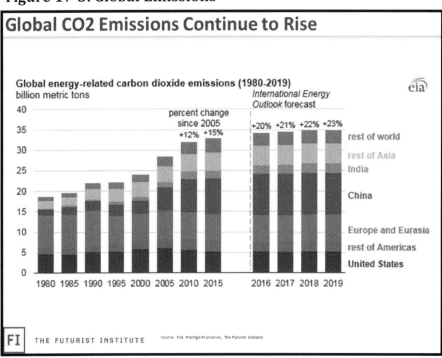

CHAPTER 18

WIND

Wind power has significant potential as a renewable energy source at scale. This is something that has been seen in areas as different as Texas and Germany and central Europe. In these places, wind has become a critical part of the energy mix.

But there are also some intermediate challenges posed by wind.

This is a function of the fact that wind tends to run at its strongest at night, which is an off-peak time for serving power loads. In other words, you get the wind power when you least need it. This is in stark contrast to solar power, which sees its peak production during the day, which matches the power load dispatch, because on-peak times are during the day.

In other words, you get solar power exactly when you need it.

But as with wind, solar is more predictable and reliable in some areas than others.

In Figure 18-1, you can see an illustrative example I created of a power cost curve. The one thing you will notice is that wind sometimes dispatches at negative prices. This can happen at night, and it is something referred to in the power market as negative wind swing. It impacted the Texas power market for a number of years.

Since wind power has been subsidized, power producers do not care if wind power prices are negative at night. After all, the subsidies help make wind power profitable even in such instances. But there is a bigger challenge for the entire power grid. Because power is dispatched at the marginal price. So, a negative price for wind at night makes all power on the grid dispatch at negative prices.

Figure 18-1: Illustrative Wind Cost Curve[1]

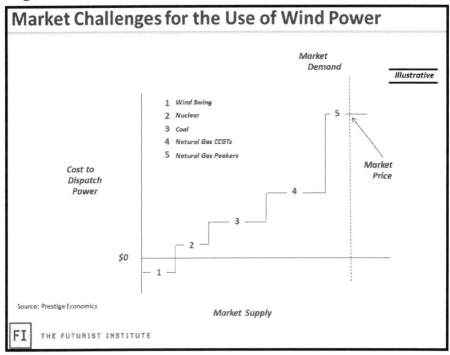

In power markets where wind prices dispatch negative, this can threaten to kick off the baseload, where coal plants eventually need to be shut down, rather than dispatch non-subsidized negative power prices all night long.

This has impacted coal-fired power generation plants in ERCOT, which is roughly the power region for Texas. And it has hastened a switch to natural gas-fired power generation in Texas. The reason the impact was so significant is that wind power is heavily concentrated in Texas, which has more than three times the wind generation capacity of the next two states that generate the most wind power. These dynamics can be seen in Figure 18-2.

Figure 18-2: U.S. Wind Power Generation by State[2]

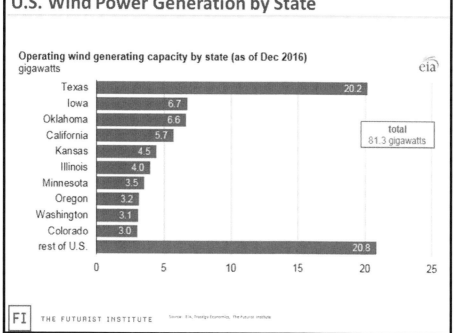

Looking Ahead

In the decade ahead, wind power generation is likely to rise in the United States. In Figure 18-3, you can see the trend higher in wind power generation, which had more than doubled between 2011 and 2017. But even in 2018, total U.S. wind power generation represented only 6.6 percent of total power generation.[3] In other words, it is a small percentage of the total. And even though we expect U.S. wind power generation to rise, it is likely to remain a relatively low percentage.

We expect U.S. wind power generation will continue to rise in the coming decade. And we expect wind power generation will continue to rise in Europe and globally. But generally speaking, we expect wind power to be a low percent of total global power.

Figure 18-3: Wind Power Generation[4]

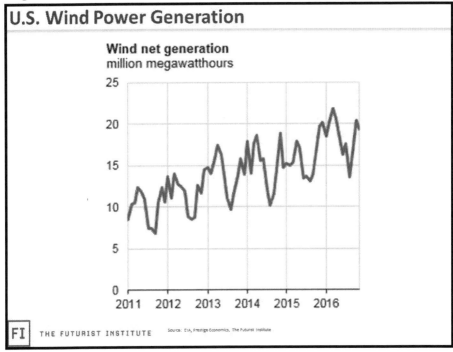

CHAPTER 19

SOLAR

As with wind power, solar power generation has risen — and it is likely to continue to rise on trend in the United States and abroad. But solar power is starting from a very low level of total power generation in the United States and globally.

To put this in perspective, solar is a very small part of the total power generation mix in the United States. In 2018, solar power generation represented only 2.3 percent of total U.S. power generation.[1] This is compared to 27.4 percent of power generation from coal or 35.1 percent of power generation from natural gas.

In recent years, significant strides have been made in solar power generation. And as compared to nuclear power generation, which I discuss in Chapter 23, solar power is on the rise. In Figure 19-1, you can see the trend increase in U.S. solar power generation, which has risen significantly over the past decade.

Looking Ahead

Solar power generation will continue to rise on trend in the decade ahead. But it is still likely to remain a relatively small part of the overall U.S. energy power mix.

Many decades ahead, however, solar is likely to become more important as part of a mix of the myriad sources of U.S. power. Another major change for solar power in the decade ahead is that more small-scale solar PV capacity will be connected to the U.S. grid.

On a global basis, solar power generation is also likely to rise in the decade ahead. But global solar is also likely to remain relatively low in absolute and percentage terms.

Figure 19-1: U.S. Solar Power Generation[2]

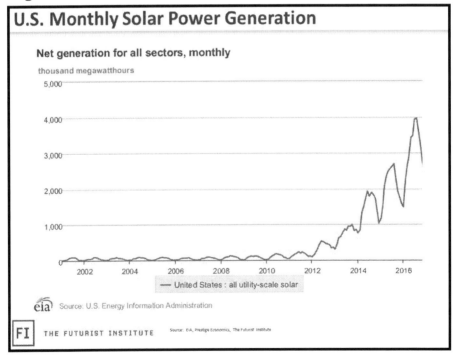

CHAPTER 20

HYDROELECTRIC AND GEOTHERMAL POWER

I have intentionally lumped geothermal and hydroelectric energy sources together because they have one major thing in common: limited opportunities for use, at least in their current forms. Yes, there are attempts to capture tidal wave movements, but those are still at relatively early levels of testing and deployment.

But damming up rivers to create massive lakes is becoming harder and harder as global populations increase. This is a fundamental reality that cannot be stemmed easily. It also explains why U.S. hydroelectric power production has been relatively unchanged for decades, which you can see in Figure 20-1.

Similarly, finding new specialized geologic opportunities to tap into cheap and renewable geothermal energy are also not likely to pop up. This means that while renewable biomass, wind, and solar power generation are likely to increase significantly over time, the same really cannot be said about hydroelectric and geothermal power.

It's ironic that hydro and geothermal are two of the very first power sources humans tapped into, but it now appears without a major technological step change and revolution of some sort, they can go no further.

And even with some form of revolutionary tech emerging on the horizon, it would take time for a material impact to occur, and that would likely be in a time window beyond the decade ahead.

But for the foreseeable future, these are likely to become relatively less important sources of electric power. Of course, despite its declining percentage of U.S. power generation, hydro still represents about twice as much power generation as solar power.

Figure 20-1: Hydroelectric Power Generation[1]

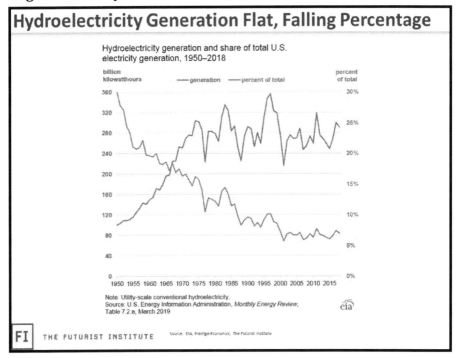

In Figure 20-1, you can see how hydroelectricity has fallen as a percentage of U.S. power generation for decades — since 1950.

Similarly, in Figure 20-2, you can see the sources of geothermal power in the United States, which are limited to a handful of mountain and Pacific states.

Looking Ahead

Without a major revolution in these forms of energy, they are likely to remain very small percentages of U.S. and global power production. The biggest renewable opportunities are likely to be elsewhere. After all, the sun shines and the wind blows in a lot more places than you can dam rivers or access geothermic activities.

Figure 20-2: Geothermal Power in the Western United States[2]

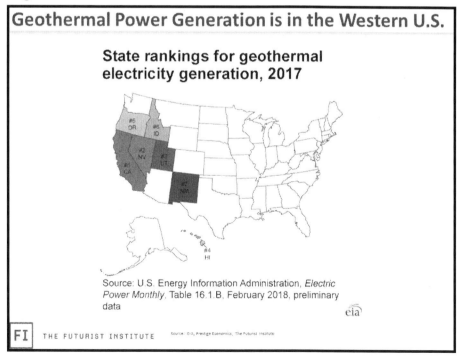

CHAPTER 21

WASTE TO ENERGY

Waste to energy is the creation of power by burning solid municipal waste. It's not quite a renewable energy and it's not exactly a clean form of energy, but burning solid municipal waste to generate energy can reduce the total overall environmental impact of solid waste that would otherwise sit in landfills or might be dumped into the sea.

In 2015, 262 million tons of solid waste were burned. The type of waste was distributed among a number of different waste categories, but paper was a plurality of the waste material, at almost 26 percent of U.S. waste.[1] The next most important solid waste categories were food waste, at over 15 percent, and yard trimmings and plastics, at just over 13 percent of total solid waste each.

Solid waste electricity capacity in the United States is at a relatively low level, and it has remained relatively unchanged since the mid-1990s, as you can see in Figure 21-1.

Compared to a number of other countries, the United States burns a relatively low percentage of its total municipal solid waste. This is due, in part, to a few relatively regional concentrations of waste-to-energy facilities in the United States.

In Japan, 68 percent of total municipal solid waste is burned with energy recovery. Germany burns 25 percent of its total municipal solid waste. But in the United States, only about 13 percent of total municipal solid waste is burned for energy.[2]

In Figure 21-2, you can see comparative rates of burning total municipal solid waste for energy across countries.

Figure 21-1: Solid Waste Power Generation Capacity[3]

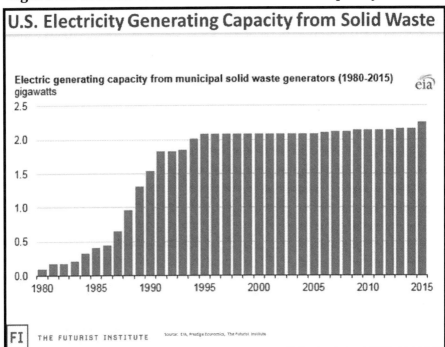

Looking Ahead

On a global basis, power generation from solid waste is likely to increase. This is especially true as emerging economies grow and generate more solid waste. As the population of planet Earth rises by over 2 billion in the next 30 years, land will become a more valuable asset — and it will be priced at a premium.

Figure 21-2: Solid Waste Burned by Country[4]

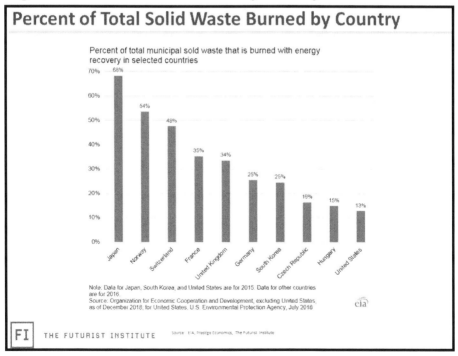

CHAPTER 22

HYDROGEN

About 15 years ago, I was at an alternative energy conference, and the topic of hydrogen fuel cells came up in discussions with some of the scientists on-site. The biggest challenge then was that hydrogen fuel cell vehicles would require the engine block to be essentially coated in platinum as a catalyst to turn hydrogen into fuel.

There was talk of renting out the engine blocks and fuel cells, but there was concern that they would be so valuable that they would become easy targets for theft.

At the time, and for years thereafter, I used to joke that it sounded like a very expensive way to "pimp your ride." This is especially true considering the relatively low cost of petroleum fuels.

As you can imagine, the platinum issue has been the focus of research for some time, with an interest in both finding substitutes and reducing the quantity of platinum or using some form of alloy to reduce the amount of platinum required.

At the end of 2018, there were reports of some potentially significant recent strides made in experimentation in this direction.[1] But the cost of the platinum isn't the only cost issue when it comes to hydrogen fuel cell vehicles.

And here is also the cost of the hydrogen fuel. Unlike electric vehicles, which are a lot cheaper to refuel than gasoline vehicles or sometimes even free, hydrogen vehicles cost a lot more to fuel up. In fact, according to the California Fuel Cell Partnership, "Hydrogen fuel prices range from $12.85 to more than $16 per kilogram (kg), but the most common price is $13.99 per kg (equivalent on a price per energy basis to $5.60 per gallon of gasoline), which translates to an operating cost of $0.21 per mile."[2] In order to defray these costs early on, some automakers included three years of hydrogen fuel with their initial sales and lease offerings to mitigate some of these costs.[3]

But even if the hydrogen were cheap, there is still currently a lack of infrastructure. And without a way to fuel up, this could slow adoption of hydrogen fuel cell vehicles.

Looking Ahead

There are significant challenges ahead for hydrogen fuel cell technology. As in other areas of energy development, relatively high costs compared to hydrocarbons as well as a lack of infrastructure will be critical. Over time, these challenges may be resolved, but in the decade ahead, hydrogen fuel cell vehicles are likely to see relatively limited deployment. Meanwhile, industrial hydrogen fuel cell power use may also be relatively slow in the decade ahead for the same cost and infrastructure reasons.

CHAPTER 23

ETHANOL

A recent article noted that hydrogen fuel cell vehicles "appear dead" because of the rise of electric vehicles.[1]

But one kind of alternative fuel vehicle that is far from dead — and is currently the majority of the U.S. alternative vehicle fleet — are ethanol vehicles. In fact, in 2017, 79 percent of all U.S. alternative fuel vehicles were ethanol vehicles.[2] But the outlook for growth in alternative fuel vehicles does not favor ethanol vehicles, even though ethanol will remain a critical part of the fuel mix. Ethanol vehicles, although at risk of being squeezed out by electric vehicles, will remain important in the decade to come — and well beyond as part of the fleet.

Ethanol vehicles are set to lose alternative vehicle market share to electric vehicles through 2050. But electric vehicles will only equal ethanol vehicles as a percent of alternative vehicles by 2037, according to EIA forecasts. In that year, the EIA predicts both electric vehicles and ethanol vehicles will be about one-third of the total fleet stock of alternative vehicles.[3]

Looking Ahead

In the decade ahead, and indeed until 2037, ethanol vehicles are expected to remain the plurality of alternative vehicles. Thereafter, ethanol vehicles are still expected to remain a critical part of the alternative vehicle fleet. Even as late as 2050, 16 million ethanol vehicles are expected be part of the fleet — or about 23 percent of alternative vehicles. In contrast, electric vehicles are expected to be about 32 million vehicles, or 43 percent, of the forecasted 73 million alternative vehicle fleet. But that 73 million represents just about 25 percent of the total fleet of 295 million vehicles. This means that alternatives are likely to remain a relatively small part of a largely hydrocarbon-fueled fleet. It also means that ethanol as an additive is likely to be even more important in the future of energy to stretch oil molecules.[4]

Figure 23-1: Ethanol and EV Proportion of U.S. Alternatives[5]

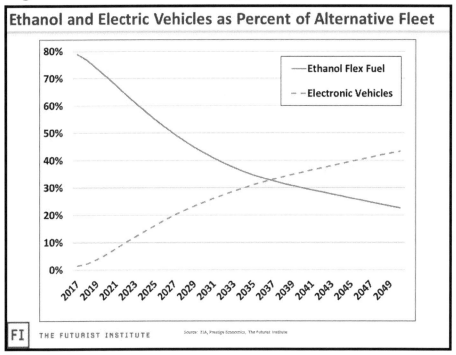

Ethanol and Electric Vehicles as Percent of Alternative Fleet

CHAPTER 24

NUCLEAR POWER

Nuclear power is a critical part of the baseload of electric power generation for a number of countries, including the United States. Nevertheless, we expect that nuclear power is likely to remain a relatively low percentage of global power production, even though power production is projected to increase.

Nuclear power generation is likely to remain relatively low for several critical reasons. On the one hand, setting up new greenfield nuclear facilities is challenging from a capital intensity and permitting standpoint. And on the other hand, there are challenges in terms of managing nuclear waste.

Events like Chernobyl and Three Mile Island may be far in the past for most, but the Fukushima nuclear disaster was just in 2011 — and it highlighted the risks to nuclear facilities and infrastructure.

U.S. nuclear power generation has remained relatively stable for decades, as you can see in Figure 24-1.

But because of cheap natural gas and a rising spent-fuel problem, nuclear power generation capacity is expected to fall in the United States in the decade ahead, as shown in Figure 24-1.

As for the spent nuclear fuel issue, the problem can be seen in Figure 24-2. Although nuclear power is clean from a carbon footprint standpoint, the environmental footprint and total impact may be quite large indeed, unless spent nuclear fuel issues can be resolved.

On a global basis, the Unites States remains the top producer of nuclear power, followed by France, China, and Russia. U.S. nuclear power generation is twice as great as French and more than three times greater than Chinese capacity.[1]

Figure 24-1: U.S. Nuclear Power Generation[2]

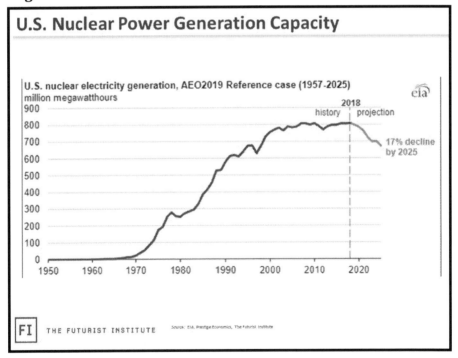

Looking Ahead

In the decade ahead, nuclear power will remain an important part of the power baseload in countries where it exists. In the United States, for example, it was 19.3 percent of total power generation in 2018.[3]

Additionally, in the decade ahead, we expect some foreign countries will add nuclear power capacity, especially China, which is planning to start construction on 11 new nuclear power plants in 2019 and 2020 alone.[4] If the spent fuel issue can be managed or resolved, the outlook for nuclear would be even stronger — despite the capital intensity of greenfield nuclear power plant projects.

Figure 24-2: Metric Tons of U.S. Spent Nuclear Fuel[5]

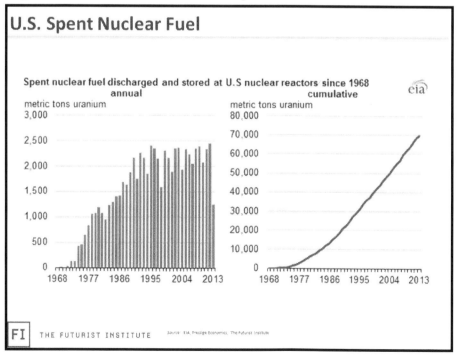

Pulling Everything Together

THE FUTURE OF ENERGY

My main goal in writing this book was to help you think about the future of energy. As you can now hopefully see, there are some critical dynamics that are going to drive the global energy situation. The reality of a rising global population and rising real GDP per capita in emerging markets will be at the top of the list.

But those aren't the only important dynamics that will drive energy in the decade ahead. From a technology standpoint, energy companies must start to implement better data analysis, automation, and other cost-saving tools to improve efficiency and reduce costs, or they will get left behind. Every company that wants to survive and thrive in the current era of disruption must be a technology company. That goes for energy companies too.

One question that's often discussed among commodity experts is whether there's another China. There isn't another China that will emerge in the next 30 years, but another 2 billion people will come to exist on this planet. So, in some respects, there are another two Chinas coming. You can see this in World Bank population forecasts through 2050, back in Figure 4-1.

This increase in population will drastically drive up demand for oil, natural gas, coal, power, and renewables. Plus, given still relatively low levels of global wealth, there is still more China to come — and there is India, the rest of emerging Asia, and other emerging markets. As emerging market wealth rises, energy demand will rise across energy sectors and types.

While some industries are on the edge of virtual technology revolutions, energy is industry-driven and impacted by the physical limitations of gravity and distance in the real world — not just a virtual one. And some changes in energy technology will be limited by the chemistry of batteries and the fuel efficiency of carbon chain molecules, as well as the rules of gravity and the reality of power load serving.

The inherent challenges posed by our physical reality underscore why energy changes in the decade ahead may be more marginal in terms of adoption rates, efficiency, and clean tech. Demand will rise for all kinds of energy. In wealthy economies, the mix will shift to renewables. And while the number of electric vehicles is poised to rise, oil is likely to remain king for a long time to come — and it is only likely to become much more important on a global basis in the decade ahead.

Investments and Options

From a financial market and institutional investor standpoint, Environmental, social, and governance (ESG) investors who are focused on environmental issues, climate change, and clean power will continue to drive investment into these sectors to meet their sustainability, alternative energy, clean technology, or other related investor mandates.

Despite these ESG goals, on a global scale, there is another ethical issue at play. If energy is made too expensive for some emerging economies, then these historically impoverished or disadvantaged economies may never have the opportunity to experience growth.

There is a great quote that seems apropos here. In Berthold Brecht's play *Die Dreigroschenoper*, there is a quote about morality and income. Two of the lead characters state, *"Erst kommt das Fressen. Dann kommt die Moral."* This roughly translates to "First comes the feeding. Then come the morals."[1]

For emerging markets, this is the best way to typify their likely approach to hydrocarbons — and most specifically coal — as well as all forms of energy in the decade ahead.

It means that clean energy — or at least cleaner energy — could largely remain the option of more developed economies in the decade ahead.

Further Learning
If you've enjoyed this book and want to learn more about the future of energy and how to incorporate new and emerging technology risks and opportunities into your strategic planning, I would recommend pursuing the Futurist and Long-Term Analyst (FLTA) training program that I created for The Futurist Institute.

All the details about the FLTA can be found at
www.futuristinstitute.org.

ENDNOTES

Chapter 3

1. Manfreda, J. (13 April 2015). "The Real History of Fracking." *Oilprice.com*. Retrieved on 10 May 2019 from https://oilprice.com/Energy/Crude-Oil/The-Real-History-Of-Fracking.html.
2. Image sourced from Adobe Stock.
3. "Tight Oil Production Estimates by Play." Energy Information Agency. Retrieved on 10 May 2019 from https://www.eia.gov/petroleum/data.php#crude.
4. "The U.S. Gulf Coast Became a Net Exporter of Crude Oil in Late 2018." (18 March 2019). Energy Information Agency. Retrieved on 10 May 2019 from https://www.eia.gov/todayinenergy/detail.php?id=38732.
5. "Shale Oil and Shale Gas Resources are Globally Abundant." (2 January 2014). Energy Information Agency. Retrieved on 10 May 2019 from https://www.eia.gov/todayinenergy/detail.php?id=14431.

Chapter 4

1. Population Estimates and Projections. The World Bank. Retrieved on 10 May 2019 from https://datacatalog.worldbank.org/dataset/population-estimates-and-projections.
2. Ibid.
3. Ibid.
4. World Oil Outlook 2018. OPEC. Retrieved on 9 May 2019 from https://woo.opec.org/chapter.html?chapterNr=1&chartID=9. All OPEC data and graphs provided with permission. We very much appreciate the rights to use these.
5. World Oil Outlook 2018. OPEC. Retrieved on 9 May 2019 from https://woo.opec.org/chapter.html?chapterNr=3&chartID=39.
6. World Oil Outlook 2018. OPEC. Retrieved on 9 May 2019 from https://woo.opec.org/chapter.html?chapterNr=3&chartID=122.
7. "China Surpassed the United States as the World's Largest Crude Oil Importer in 2017." (5 February 2018). Retrieved on 10 May 2019 from https://www.eia.gov/todayinenergy/detail.php?id=34812.
8. Ibid.
9. Data from Markit and Econoday. Analysis performed by Prestige Economics.
10. Data from eSignal. Analysis performed by Prestige Economics.

Chapter 5

1. Energy Information Agency. Retrieved on 9 May 2019 from https://www.eia.gov/oil_gas/rpd/shale_gas.pdf .
2. Annual Energy Outlook 2019. (24 January 2019). Energy Information Agency. Retrieved on 9 May 2019 from https://www.eia.gov/outlooks/aeo/.
3. Energy Information Agency. Retrieved on 9 May 2019 from https://www.eia.gov/tools/faqs/faq.php?id=73&t=11.

Chapter 6

1. Prestige Economics forecasts.
2. Energy Information Agency.
3. Annual Energy Outlook 2019. (24 January 2019). Energy Information Agency. Retrieved on 9 May 2019 from https://www.eia.gov/outlooks/aeo/.

Chapter 7

1. Annual Energy Outlook 2019. (24 January 2019). Energy Information Agency. Retrieved on 9 May 2019 from https://www.eia.gov/outlooks/aeo/.

2. World Oil Outlook 2018. OPEC. Retrieved on 9 May 2019 from https://woo.opec.org/chapter.html?chapterNr=2&chartID=14.

3. World Oil Outlook 2018. OPEC. Retrieved on 9 May 2019 from https://woo.opec.org/chapter.html?chapterNr=2&chartID=15

Chapter 8

1. Google Trends U.S. web search for "Electric Vehicles." Retrieved on 9 May 2019.

2. Google Trends worldwide web search for "Electric Vehicles." Retrieved on 9 May 2019.

3. Annual Energy Outlook 2019. (24 January 2019). Energy Information Agency. Retrieved on 9 May 2019 from https://www.eia.gov/outlooks/aeo/tables_ref.php.

4. World Oil Outlook 2018. OPEC. Retrieved on 9 May 2019 from https://woo.opec.org/chapter.html?chapterNr=3&chartID=54.

5. Ibid.

6. World Oil Outlook 2018. OPEC. Retrieved on 9 May 2019 from https://woo.opec.org/chapter.html?chapterNr=3&chartID=52.

7. Bennet, J. (November 2015). "We Need an Energy Miracle." *The Atlantic*. Retrieved on 9 May 2019 from https://www.theatlantic.com/magazine/archive/2015/11/we-need-an-energy-miracle/407881/.

8. Boyle, A. (5 March 2019). "Bill Gates-backed Breakthrough Energy Ventures Supports KoBold's Cobalt Quest." GeekWire. Retrieved on 9 May 2019 from https://www.geekwire.com/2019/bill-gates-backed-breakthrough-energy-ventures-backs-cobalt-hunters-kobold-metals/.

9. Ibid.

10. Prices from LME and Trading Economics. Analysis by Prestige Economics.

11. Reisinger, D. (21 February 2018). "Here's Why Apple Wants to Buy Cobalt Directly From Miners." *Fortune*. Retrieved on 9 May 2019 from http://fortune.com/2018/02/21/apple-buy-cobalt-miners/.

12. Prices from Statista. Analysis by Prestige Economics. Retrieved on 9 May 2019 from https://www.statista.com/statistics/606350/battery-grade-lithium-carbonate-price/

13. Bullard, N. "Electric Car Price Tag Shrinks Along With Battery Cost." *Bloomberg Opinion*. Retrieved on 9 May 2019 from https://www.bloomberg.com/opinion/articles/2019-04-12/electric-vehicle-battery-shrinks-and-so-does-the-total-cost.

14. Bennet, J.

15. Energy Information Agency. Retrieved on 9 May 2019 from https://www.eia.gov/tools/faqs/faq.php?id=73&t=11.

Chapter 9

1. U.S. Census Bureau, E-Commerce Retail Sales [ECOMSA], retrieved from FRED, Federal Reserve Bank of St. Louis; https://fred.stlouisfed.org/series/ECOMSA, May 11, 2019.

2. U.S. Census Bureau, E-Commerce Retail Sales as a Percent of Total Sales [ECOMPCTSA], retrieved from FRED, Federal Reserve Bank of St. Louis; https://fred.stlouisfed.org/series/ECOMPCTSA, May 11, 2019.

3. U.S. Federal Highway Administration, Vehicle Miles Traveled [TRFVOLUSM227NFWA], retrieved from FRED, Federal Reserve Bank of St. Louis; https://fred.stlouisfed.org/series/TRFVOLUSM227NFWA, May 11, 2019.

4. Statista. Retrieved on 11 May 2019 from https://www.statista.com/statistics/534123/e-commerce-share-of-retail-sales-worldwide/.

Chapter 10

1. "2017 State of Telecommuting in the U.S. Employee Workforce." Flexjobs. Retrieved on 9 May 2019 from https://www.flexjobs.com/2017-State-of-Telecommuting-US.

2. Ibid.

Chapter 11

1. Energy Information Agency. (6 December 2017). "Nearly Half of All U.S. Electricity Customers Have Smart Meters." Retrieved on 9 May 2011 from https://www.eia.gov/todayinenergy/detail.php?id=34012.
2. Ibid.
3. Ibid.
4. European Commission. "Smart Metering Deployment in the European Union." Retrieved on 9 May 2019 from https://ses.jrc.ec.europa.eu/smart-metering-deployment-european-union.
5. Energy Information Agency. (6 December 2017). "Nearly Half of All U.S. Electricity Customers Have Smart Meters." Retrieved on 9 May 2011 from https://www.eia.gov/todayinenergy/detail.php?id=34012.

Chapter 17

1. Google Trends U.S. web search for "Climate Change." Retrieved on 9 May 2019.
2. Google Trends worldwide web search for "Climate Change." Retrieved on 9 May 2019.
3. "U.S. Energy-Related CO2 Emissions Expected to Rise Slightly in 2018, Remain Flat in 2019. Energy Information Agency. Retrieved on 9 May 2019 from https://www.eia.gov/todayinenergy/detail.php?id=34872.

Chapter 18

1. Prestige Economics analysis.
2. Energy Information Agency. Retrieved on 9 May 2019 from https://www.eia.gov/todayinenergy/detail.php?id=31032.
3. "Energy Power Monthly." (February 2019). Energy Information Agency. Retrieved on 9 May 2019 from https://www.eia.gov/electricity/monthly/.
4. Annual Energy Outlook 2019. (24 January 2019). Energy Information Agency. Retrieved on 9 May 2019 from https://www.eia.gov/outlooks/aeo/tables_ref.php .

Chapter 19

1. "Energy Power Monthly." (February 2019). Energy Information Agency,. Retrieved on 9 May 2019 from https://www.eia.gov/electricity/monthly/.
2. Energy Information Agency.

Chapter 20

1. Annual Energy Outlook 2019. (24 January 2019). Energy Information Agency. Retrieved on 9 May 2019 from https://www.eia.gov/outlooks/aeo/tables_ref.php.
2. "Electric Power Monthly." (February 2018.) Energy Information Agency.

Chapter 21

1. "Biomass Explained." Energy Information Agency. Retrieved on 9 May 2019 from https://www.eia.gov/energyexplained/index.php?page=biomass_waste_to_energy#tab1.
2. "Biomass Explained." Energy Information Agency. Retrieved on 9 May 2019 from https://www.eia.gov/energyexplained/index.php?page=biomass_waste_to_energy#tab2.
3 . "Waste-to-Energy Electricity Generation Concentrated in Florida and Northeast." (8 April 2016). Energy Information Agency. Retrieved on 9 May 2019 from https://www.eia.gov/todayinenergy/detail.php?id=25732.
4. "Biomass Explained." Energy Information Agency. Retrieved on 9 May 2019 from https://www.eia.gov/energyexplained/index.php?page=biomass_waste_to_energy#tab2.

Chapter 22

1. Dyson, T. (26 December 2018). "Researchers Find Alternative to Pure Platinum Catalyst for Hydrogen Fuel Cells." *UPI*. Retrieved on 9 May 2019 from https://www.upi.com/Science_News/2018/12/26/Researchers-find-alternative-to-pure-platinum-catalyst-for-hydrogen-fuel-cells/7261545839062/ and Sagoff, J. (13 December 2019). "Scientists Maximize the Effectiveness of Platinum in Fuel Cells." Phys.org. Retrieved on 9 May 2019 from https://phys.org/news/2018-12-scientists-maximize-effectiveness-platinum-fuel.html.
2. "Cost to Refill." California Fuel Cell Partnership. Retrieved on 9 May 2019 from https://cafcp.org/content/cost-refill.
3. Ibid.

Chapter 23

1. Hoium, T. (23 April 2019). "Hydrogen Cars Appear Dead as EVs Take the Reins." *The Motley Fool.* Retrieved on 9 May 2019 from https://www.fool.com/investing/2019/04/23/hydrogen-cars-appear-dead-as-evs-take-the-reins.aspx.
2. Annual Energy Outlook 2019. (24 January 2019). Energy Information Agency. Retrieved on 9 May 2019 from https://www.eia.gov/outlooks/aeo/tables_ref.php .
3. Ibid.
4. Ibid.
5. Ibid.

Chapter 24

1. "Nuclear Power in the World Today." (February 2019). World Nuclear Association. Retrieved on 9 May 2019 from http://www.world-nuclear.org/information-library/current-and-future-generation/nuclear-power-in-the-world-today.aspx.
2. "Despite Closures, U.S. Nuclear Electricity Generation in 2018 Surpassed its Previous Peak." (21 March 2019). Energy Information Agency. Retrieved on 9 May 2019 from https://www.eia.gov/todayinenergy/detail.php?id=38792.
3. "Energy Power Monthly." (February 2019). Energy Information Agency. Retrieved on 9 May 2019 from https://www.eia.gov/electricity/monthly/.
4. "Plans for New Reactors Worldwide." (April 2019). World Nuclear Association. Retrieved on 9 May 2019 from http://www.world-nuclear.org/information-library/current-and-future-generation/plans-for-new-reactors-worldwide.aspx.
5. "Updated EIA Survey Provides Data on Spent Nuclear Fuel in The United States." (8 December 2015.) Energy Information Agency. Retrieved on 9 May 2019 from https://www.eia.gov/todayinenergy/detail.php?id=24052.

Conclusion

1. Brecht, B. (1928). *Die Dreigroschenoper*. Translation by Jason Schenker.

ABOUT THE AUTHOR

Jason Schenker is the President of Prestige Economics and the world's top-ranked financial market futurist. Bloomberg News has ranked Mr. Schenker the #1 forecaster in the world in 25 categories since 2011, including for his forecasts of crude oil prices, natural gas prices, the euro, the pound, the Swiss franc, the Chinese RMB, gold prices, industrial metals prices, agricultural prices, U.S. non-farm payrolls, and U.S. home sales.

Mr. Schenker has written 15 books and compiled two almanacs. Five of his books have been #1 Best Sellers on Amazon, including *Commodity Prices 101*, *Recession-Proof*, *Electing Recession*, *Quantum: Computing Nouveau*, and *Jobs for Robots*. He also edited and compiled the #1 Best Seller *The Robot and Automation Almanac — 2018* as well as the 2019 edition of the almanac. Mr. Schenker is also a columnist for *Bloomberg Opinion*, and he has appeared as a guest host on Bloomberg Television as well as a guest on CNBC and other television media. He is frequently quoted in the press, including *The Wall Street Journal*, *The New York Times*, and *The Financial Times*.

Prior to founding Prestige Economics, Mr. Schenker worked for McKinsey & Company as a Risk Specialist, where he directed trading and risk initiatives on six continents. Before joining McKinsey, Mr. Schenker worked for Wachovia as an Economist.

Mr. Schenker holds a Master's in Applied Economics from UNC Greensboro, a Master's in Negotiation from CSU Dominguez Hills, a Master's in German from UNC Chapel Hill, and a Bachelor's with distinction in History and German from The University of Virginia. He also holds a certificate in FinTech from MIT, an executive certificate in Supply Chain Management from MIT, a graduate certificate in Professional Development from UNC, a certificate in Negotiation from Harvard Law School, and a certificate in Cybersecurity from Carnegie Mellon University.

Mr. Schenker holds the professional designations ERP® (Energy Risk Professional), CMT® (Chartered Market Technician), CVA® (Certified Valuation Analyst), CFP® (Certified Financial Planner), and FLTA™ (Certified Futurist and Long-Term Analyst). Mr. Schenker is also an instructor for LinkedIn Learning. His courses include Financial Risk Management, Recession-Proof Strategies, Audit and Due Diligence, and a weekly Economic Indicator Series.

Mr. Schenker is a member of the Texas Business Leadership Council, the only CEO-based public policy research organization in Texas, with a limited membership of 100 CEOs and Presidents. He is also a 2018 Board of Director member of the Texas Lyceum, a non-partisan, nonprofit that fosters business and policy dialogue on important U.S. and Texas issues. He is also the VP of Technology for the Texas Lyceum Executive Committee.

Mr. Schenker is an active executive in FinTech. He has been a member of the Central Texas Angel Network and he advises multiple startups and nonprofits. He is also a member of the National Association of Corporate Directors as well as an NACD Board Governance Fellow.

In October 2016, Mr. Schenker founded The Futurist Institute to help consultants, strategists, and executives become futurists through an online and in-person training and certification program. Participants can earn the Certified Futurist and Long-Term Analyst™ — FLTA™ — designation.

Mr. Schenker was ranked one of the top 100 most influential financial advisors in the world by Investopedia in June 2018.

For more information about Jason Schenker:
www.jasonschenker.com

For more information about The Futurist Institute:
www.futuristinstitute.org

For more information about Prestige Economics:
www.prestigeeconomics.com

TOP FORECASTER ACCURACY RANKINGS

Prestige Economics has been recognized as the most accurate independent commodity and financial market research firm in the world. As the only forecaster for Prestige Economics, Jason Schenker is very proud that Bloomberg News has ranked him a top forecaster in 43 different categories since 2011, including #1 in the world in 25 different forecast categories.

Mr. Schenker has been top ranked as a forecaster of economic indicators, energy prices, metals prices, agricultural prices, and foreign exchange rates.

ECONOMIC TOP RANKINGS

#1 Non-Farm Payroll Forecaster in the World
#1 New Home Sales Forecaster in the World
#2 U.S. Unemployment Rate Forecaster in the World
#3 Durable Goods Orders Forecaster in the World
#6 Consumer Confidence Forecaster in the World
#7 ISM Manufacturing Index Forecaster in the World
#7 U.S. Housing Start Forecaster in the World

ENERGY PRICE TOP RANKINGS

#1 WTI Crude Oil Price Forecaster in the World

#1 Brent Crude Oil Price Forecaster in the World

#1 Henry Hub Natural Gas Price Forecaster in the World

METALS PRICE TOP RANKINGS

#1 Gold Price Forecaster in the World

#1 Platinum Price Forecaster in the World

#1 Palladium Price Forecaster in the World

#1 Industrial Metals Price Forecaster in the World

#1 Copper Price Forecaster in the World

#1 Aluminum Price Forecaster in the World

#1 Nickel Price Forecaster in the World

#1 Tin Price Forecaster in the World

#1 Zinc Price Forecaster in the World

#2 Precious Metals Price Forecaster in the World

#2 Silver Price Forecaster in the World

#2 Lead Price Forecaster in the World

#2 Iron Ore Forecaster in the World

AGRICULTURAL PRICE TOP RANKINGS

#1 Coffee Price Forecaster in the World

#1 Cotton Price Forecaster in the World

#1 Sugar Price Forecaster in the World

#1 Soybean Price Forecaster in the World

FOREIGN EXCHANGE TOP RANKINGS

#1 Euro Forecaster in the World

#1 British Pound Forecaster in the World

#1 Swiss Franc Forecaster in the World

#1 Chinese RMB Forecaster in the World

#1 Russian Ruble Forecaster in the World

#1 Brazilian Real Forecaster in the World

#2 Turkish Lira Forecaster in the World

#3 Major Currency Forecaster in the World

#3 Canadian Dollar Forecaster in the World

#4 Japanese Yen Forecaster in the World

#5 Australian Dollar Forecaster in the World

#7 Mexican Peso Forecaster in the World

#1 EURCHF Forecaster in the World

#2 EURJPY Forecaster in the World

#2 EURGBP Forecaster in the World

#2 EURRUB Forecaster in the World

For more information about Prestige Economics:

www.prestigeeconomics.com

PUBLISHER

Prestige Professional Publishing LLC was founded in 2011 to produce insightful and timely professional reference books. We are registered with the Library of Congress.

Published Titles

Be the Shredder, Not the Shred
Commodity Prices 101
Electing Recession
Financial Risk Management Fundamentals
Futureproof Supply Chain
A Gentle Introduction to Audit and Due Diligence
Jobs for Robots
Midterm Economics
The Fog of Data
The Promise of Blockchain
Quantum: Computing Nouveau
Robot-Proof Yourself
Spikes: Growth Hacking Leadership
The Future of Energy
The Robot and Automation Almanac — 2018
The Robot and Automation Almanac — 2019

Future Titles

Reading the Economic Tea Leaves
The Dumpster Fire Election
The Future of Finance is Now
The Future of Project Management
The Robot and Automation Almanac — 2020

DISCLAIMER

FROM THE PUBLISHER

The following disclaimer applies to any content in this book:

This book is commentary intended for general information use only and is not investment advice. Prestige Professional Publishing LLC does not make recommendations on any specific or general investments, investment types, asset classes, non-regulated markets, specific equities, bonds, or other investment vehicles. Prestige Professional Publishing LLC does not guarantee the completeness or accuracy of analyses and statements in this book, nor does Prestige Professional Publishing LLC assume any liability for any losses that may result from the reliance by any person or entity on this information. Opinions, forecasts, and information are subject to change without notice. This book does not represent a solicitation or offer of financial or advisory services or products; this book is only market commentary intended and written for general information use only. This book does not constitute investment advice. All links were correct and active at the time this book was published.

The Fog of Data addresses the rising volume of data and describes the best ways to navigate data challenges — and how to derive valuable data insights. *The Fog of Data* was published by Prestige Professional Publishing in March 2019.

Jobs for Robots provides an in-depth look at the future of automation and robots, with a focus on the opportunities as well as the risks ahead. Job creation in coming years will be extremely strong for the kind of workers that do not require payroll taxes, health care, or vacation: robots. *Jobs for Robots* was published in February 2017. This book has been a #1 Best Seller on Amazon.

Prestige Professional Publishing LLC

7101 Fig Vine Cove

Austin, Texas 78750

www.prestigeprofessionalpublishing.com

ISBN: 978-1-946197-35-1 *Paperback*
        978-1-946197-29-0 *Ebook*

Made in the USA
Middletown, DE
20 May 2019